BY CHARLES BUKOWSKI
AVAILABLE FROM ECCO

The Days Run Away Like Wild Horses Over the Hills (1969)
Post Office (1971)
Mockingbird Wish Me Luck (1972)
South of No North (1973)
Burning in Water, Drowning in Flame: Selected Poems 1955–1973 (1974)
Factotum (1975)
Love Is a Dog from Hell (1977)
Women (1978)
play the piano drunk like a percussion instrument until the fingers begin to bleed a bit (1979)
Shakespeare Never Did This (1979)
Dangling in the Tournefortia (1981)
Ham on Rye (1982)
Bring Me Your Love (1983)
Hot Water Music (1983)
There's No Business (1984)
War All the Time: Poems 1981–1984 (1984)
You Get So Alone at Times That It Just Makes Sense (1986)
The Movie: "Barfly" (1987)
The Roominghouse Madrigals: Early Selected Poems 1946–1966 (1988)
Hollywood (1989)
Septuagenarian Stew: Stories & Poems (1990)
The Last Night of the Earth Poems (1992)
Screams from the Balcony: Selected Letters 1960–1970 (1993)
Pulp (1994)
Living on Luck: Selected Letters 1960s–1970s (Volume 2) (1995)
Betting on the Muse: Poems & Stories (1996)
Bone Palace Ballet: New Poems (1997)
The Captain is Out to Lunch and the Sailors Have Taken Over the Ship (1998)
Reach for the Sun: Selected Letters 1978-1994 (Volume 3) (1999)
What Matters Most Is How Well You Walk Through the Fire: New Poems (1999)
Open All Night: New Poems (2000)
Night Torn Mad with Footsteps: New Poems (2001)
Beerspit Night and Cursing: The Correspondence of Charles Bukowski & Sheri Martinelli 1960–1967 (2001)

CHARLES BUKOWSKI

BONE PALACE BALLET

NEW POEMS

ecco

An Imprint of HarperCollinsPublishers

HarperCollins books may be purchased for educational, business, or sales promotional use. For information please e-mail the Special Markets Department at SPsales@harpercollins.com.

These poems are part of an archive of unpublished work that Charles Bukowski left to be published after his death.

First Ecco edition published in 2002.

ACKNOWLEDGMENTS

On behalf of the author, the publisher would like to thank the editors of the periodicals where some of these poems first appeared.

THE Library of Congress has catalogued a previous editions as follows:

BUKOWSKI, CHARLES. 1920-1994.
    Bone palace ballet : new poems / Charles Bukowski.
        p. cm.
    ISBN 1-57423-028-X (paper : alk. paper). —ISBN 1-57423-029-8 (cloth trade : alk. paper)
    I. Title.
PS3552.U4B66   1997
811'.54—dc21   97-12731
                                                                          CIP

19 20 21 22 LSC 20 19 18 17 16 15 14 13 12

for Dr. Ellis

table of contents

1.

2.

3.

4.

5.

BONE PALACE BALLET

1

AS YOUNG AS WE WERE
EVER GOING TO GET

God's man

we were 10 or 11 years old
when we went to see the
priest.

we knocked.
a fat, frumpy woman
answered the door.
"yes?" she asked.

"we want to see the
priest," one of us
said.
I think it was Frank
who said
it.

"Father," the woman
turned her head,
"some boys want to
see you."

"tell them to come
in," said the
priest.

"follow me," said the
fat, frumpy lady.

we followed her.
the priest was in his
study.
he was behind his
desk.
he pushed some papers
aside.

"yes, boys?"

the lady left the
room.

"well," I said.

"well," said Frank.

"yes, boys, go ahead…"

"well," said Frank, "we
wondered if God was
really there."

the Father smiled.

"but, of course, He
is."

"but where is He?"
I asked.

"haven't you boys
studied your catechism?
God is Everywhere."

"oh," said Frank.

"thank you, Father,
we just wanted to
know," I said.

"it's quite all right,
boys, I'm glad you
asked."

"thank you, Father,"
said Frank.

we both did little
bows, then

18

turned
and walked out of
the room.

the fat, frumpy lady
was waiting.
she led us down the
hall and to the
door.

we walked along the
street.

"I wonder if he's
fucking her?" Frank
asked.

I looked around for God,
then answered,
"of course, he isn't."

"but what does he do
when he gets
excited?"
asked Frank.

"he probably prays,"
I said.

"it's not the same
thing," said Frank.

"he has God," I said,
"he doesn't need
that."

"I think he's fucking
her," said Frank.

"oh yeah?"

"yeah.
why don't we go back
and ask him?"

"you go back and ask
him," I said. "you're
the one who's
curious.

"I'm afraid to,"
said Frank.

"you're afraid of God,"
I said.

"well, aren't you?"
he asked.

"sure."

we stopped then at a
red light, waiting for
traffic.
neither of us had been
to Mass for
months.
it was boring.
it was more fun
talking to the
priest.

the light changed and
we crossed
over.

not normal

when I was in grammar school
our teacher told us a story
about a sailor
who told the captain,
"the flag? I hope that I *never*
see the flag again!"
"very well," he was told,
"you will get your
wish!"
and they put him in the
hold of the sailing ship
and kept him there,
sending down his
food
and he died down there
without ever seeing the
flag again.

it was a real horror
story for the other children,
very
effective.
but it wasn't quite
as effective with
me.
I sat there thinking,
well, it's too bad
about not seeing the
flag
but the best part was
not having to see the
other people.

I didn't raise my hand to
say anything about that,
though.
that would mean that
I didn't want to see them

either.
which was true.

I looked straight forward
at the blackboard
which looked far better
than
any of
them.

classical

our English teacher in Jr. High,
Mrs. Gredis, didn't sit behind
her desk, she kept the front
desk empty and she sat on
the top of the front desk
and crossed her legs high and
we saw those long silken
legs, those magical flanks,
that shining warm flesh as she
twisted her ankles and re-
crossed her legs with those
black high-heeled shoes and
spoke of Hawthorne and
Melville and Poe and others.
we boys didn't hear a word
but English was our favorite
subject and we never spoke
badly of Mrs. Gredis, we didn't
even discuss her among our-
selves, we just sat in that
class and looked at Mrs. Gredis
and we knew that our mothers
were not like that or the girls
in the class were not like that
or even the women we saw
on the street were not like that.
nobody was like Mrs. Gredis
and Mrs. Gredis knew that too,
sitting there on that front desk,
perched in front of 20 fourteen-
year-old boys who would never
forget her
through the wars and the years,
never a lady like that
watching us as she talked,
watching us looking at her,
there was laughter in her eyes,
she smiled at us,

crossed and recrossed her legs
again and again,
the skirt slipping, inching
delicately higher and higher
as she spoke of Hawthorne and
Poe and Melville and more
until the bell rang
ending the class,
the fastest hour of our day.
thank you, Mrs. Gredis, for that
most marvelous
education, you made learning
more than
easy, thank you, Mrs.
Gredis, thank
you.

the puking lady

we were around 14, Baldy
Norman and myself.
we were sitting in the neighborhood
park around ten p.m.
drinking stolen beer.

then we saw a car drive up to the
curb.
the door opened and a lady
leaned out and vomited into
the street.
she cut loose a good
load.
she sat awhile.
then she got out of her
car
and walked into the
park.
she weaved a
bit.

"she's drunk," said
Norman, "let's fuck
her!"

"o.k.," I said.

"o.k.," said Baldy.

she was moving
through the park
walking along
unsteadily.
she was
heavy but
young,
good breasts,
nice legs,

she wobbled on
her high heels.

"I'll get her
good," said Baldy.

"I'll get her good!"
said Norman.

then she saw us
sitting on the
bench.

"oh," she said.

she moved closer,
staring.

"oh, you're just nice
young boys…"

we didn't like that.

"how about a drink,
baby?" Norman
asked.

"oh no, I've had
too much to drink,
I feel awful, I've
had a fight with my
boyfriend…"

she stood weaving
in the moonlight.

"what's he got I don't
have?" asked
Norman.

"don't get fresh!"

"come here, baby,
I got something I want
to show you,"
said Baldy.

"I'm leaving," she
said and began
walking off.

Baldy jumped up
(he was half drunk)
and followed
her.

"I got something
for you, baby!"

the lady began
running.
Baldy ran after
her.

when he attempted
to tackle her,
he missed, bounced
off her large
buttocks and fell
to the
grass.

the lady ran to
her car,
started it and
gunned off down
the street.

Baldy came walking
back toward

us.

"shit, that whore!"

he sat down with us
on the bench,
picked up his beer
can and had a
mighty slug.

"she wanted it,
she wanted it
bad," he said.

"you've got guts,
Baldy," I said.

"think she'll come
back?" Norman
asked.

"sure," said Baldy,
"she wants this
turkey neck I
got."

I don't think any of
us thought she would
be back
but we sat there
drinking the beer
and
waiting.

we were all
virgins.
but we felt very
powerful then,
sitting there smoking
cigarettes,

emptying cans of
beer.

later we would all
go home and
masturbate,
thinking about that
woman in the
park,
kissing that whiskey mouth,
her legs high in the
moonlight,
the park fountain
spewing its
water
as our parents
slept in the other
bedroom,
tired of it
all.

depression kid

I never had money but I did have a
bike
and there was little to do in the
summer but ride my bike to the
beach and back.
it was a bloody-ass haul from L.A. to
Venice
but there was nothing else.
one thing, it really built up my
legs.
I was 14 years old and I had the
most powerful legs in the
Southland, maybe.

the thing that made the
ride more exciting was to
attempt to shorten the time
it took to make the
trip.
each time I broke my own
record I'd go for a new
one.

I pedaled faster and
faster.
and that was all right
except one sunny day while
I was really pumping
along
this guy in a
red sports car
screamed at me,
"Hey, kid, watch where
the fuck you're going!"
I looked over and there
was this old guy in a late
model car,
smoking a cigar

and he had a young
blonde with him.
her long hair was blowing
in the wind.

"Up your ass!" I yelled
back.

he slowed his car down
as I pumped alongside.
he looked over at me
and said, "Would you
mind repeating
that?"

I repeated that.
the girl with her hair
blowing in the wind
looked at him and
laughed.

"I've got a good mind to
park
and beat the crap
out of you!"

"Park it!
Park it!"
I yelled.

he roared ahead
and parked at the
curb.
I parked my bike
and walked toward
him.
I had no fear.
I felt great.

I walked up to the car.
he looked at me
from the car.
he didn't get
out.
the young girl was
saying something
to him.
suddenly he
started the car
and pulled
away.

he took a right at
the corner.
I walked back to my
bike.
I got on and started
pedaling.

then he was back.
he'd circled the block.
I saw his face as he looked
at me.
I'd seldom seen such
hatred.

then he was gone
down the boulevard
out of sight with his young
girl.

I pedaled along.
I was no longer in a hurry.

to hell with the record.
I had called the guy's
card and
the girl with the long
hair was thinking of

me.

I had become a
man.

burlesque

Jimmy, Bill and I went every
Sunday.
the place was on Main Street
with photos of the girls posted
outside.
the girls weren't always the
same.
sometimes one of them
would leave.
then you'd see a girl who
had been in the chorus
line,
she'd be up there
stripping.
or you'd see a girl who
had been stripping
and she'd be back in the
chorus line,
a younger stripper having
replaced her.
there was something sad
about it all.
and it got worse
during the show,
some of
the old guys jerking
off.
the young guys never
jerked off,
it was always the old
guys,
most of them sat in
the first row
which was called
"Bald-headed
Row."

I liked the comedian

best, he was dressed in
floppy clothes, suspenders,
big shoes,
felt hat turned up in front
and back.
he was really good,
we laughed at his jokes
and antics.

the most beautiful stripper always
came on last.
and once in a while
she would show
everything.
sometimes the show was
raided.
(we were never there
when it was raided)
but when the theatre was raided
it always opened up again a
week later with the same
strippers.

we were there one time when
the most beautiful stripper showed
everything.
we couldn't believe
it.

"did you see it?"

"I saw it!"

"I saw it too!"

we walked out into the
street in
disbelief.

"I'll bet they close the

place down!"

"maybe there wasn't a
vice cop in the
audience.
sometimes
the manager
knows this and
he tells the stripper
it's safe
and then
she shows her
pussy."

"then how come they
sometimes
get caught?"

"that's because sometimes
there's a new vice squad guy there
they don't know."

"they ought to let women
show their pussies,
what harm does it
do?"

"the church is against
it."

"fuck the church."

we walked along
Main Street
as young as we were
ever going to
get.

first love

at one time
when I was 16
a few writers gave me
my only hope and
chance.

my father disliked
books and
my mother disliked
books (because my father
disliked books)
especially those I brought back
from the library:
D. H. Lawrence
Dostoevsky
Turgenev
Gorky
A. Huxley
Sinclair Lewis
others.

I had my own bedroom
but at 8 p.m.
we were all supposed to go to sleep:
"Early to bed and early to rise
makes a man healthy, wealthy and wise,"
my father would say.

"LIGHTS OUT!" he would shout.

then I would take the bed lamp
place it under the covers
and with the heat and hidden light
I would continue to read:
Ibsen
Shakespeare
Chekov
Jeffers

Thurber
Conrad Aiken
others.

they gave me a chance and some hope
in a place of no chance
no hope, no feeling.

I worked for it.
it got hot under the covers.
sometimes the sheets would begin to smoke
then I'd switch the lamp off,
hold it outside to
cool off.

without those books
I'm not quite sure
how I would have turned
out:
raving; the
murderer of the father;
idiocy;
hopelessness.

when my father shouted
"LIGHTS OUT!"
I'm sure he feared
the well-written word
immortalized
forever
in our best and
most interesting
literature.

and it was there
for me
close to me
under the covers
more woman than woman
more man than man.

I had it all
and
I took it.

mountain

in high school the classes were arranged alphabetically and Burns
was always seated behind me.
Burns: largest lad in the class of '39 but all of it was
fat.
he was a gross fat fart.

he was there on my neck, my back.
I could hear his wheezing.
I could hear him shifting his flesh about.

it was hell.
and worst of all the dumb fuck thought he was
clever.
always up to some trick.
like tapping me on the back, handing me a note,
whispering, "it's from Mary Lou... she said to pass it
to you..."

"*big boy,*" said the note, "*I want to be with you so bad! I can't
take my eyes off you!*"

then he'd poke me in the back, "hey, hey, she wants you!"

I'd ignore him.

"hey, Hank, what did the priest say when he saw birdshit in
his popcorn?"

"hey, Hank ..."

on top of that he had body odor.
he always wore the same heavy green sweater,
even on the hottest day.

after each class he'd attempt to exit with me, follow me
down the hall.

"hey, Hank, wait a minute..."

40

he was slow, he had huge feet in square-toed black
shoes. they often banged together and he'd
stumble as he walked.

he was lonely but somehow I couldn't embrace his loneliness,
he made me feel physically and mentally
ill.

I had him hanging on my neck for two years.

then one day he poked me in the back: "hey, this one's
from Caroline..."

I opened the note:
"*Henry, you are the yummy yummy man of my
dreams!*"

I turned in my seat and looked at him.
he wore round glasses with thick rims.
his red wet lips were twisted into an asinine
grin.

I said, "listen, Burns, if you ever touch me or
speak to me or even look at me again, I promise I am
going to kill you!"

Mrs. Anderson, the English teacher then said for
all to hear, "Mr. Chinaski, I'll see you after class."

afterwards she looked up at me from her
desk.

"I've watched that horseplay all term long. what do you
have to say about it?"

I didn't answer.

"Mr. Chinaski, I am going to give you an 'F' in English."

"all right..."

"you can go now."

I didn't attend English class after that but I saw Burns in
my other classes and since he didn't touch me or
speak to me and since I never saw him look at me, I
didn't have to kill him.

all I continued to hear was his wheezing.

and worse, I began to feel guilty as if I had committed a
hideous
wrong.

I felt as if I had locked him up in some terrible way, in some
dark and lonely place.

but I left him there, alone.

at my back, on my neck.

Class of Summer
'39.

field exercises

is what they called them in the
R.O.T.C.
in the hills and fields on the
hottest summer days,
the Reds vs. Blues,
we had rifles but no bullets
and the officers had wooden sabers
and we'd run forward and
dive on our bellies,
take cover behind brush
while the general stood on the
hill,
he would be the final
judge as to who
won.
they were teaching us
how to kill each
other.
but the funniest thing was
when the opposing sides
happened to come upon
one another
unexpectedly,
the Reds and the Blues
(what told us apart were
the colored ribbons on
our rifles).
but I had long ago
torn mine off,
and we closed in
upon each other, got
excited,
began using rifle
butts
and the officers swung
their sabers about
each claiming victory
and there were bloody

noses, fractured skulls.
one broken arm
and I sat under a
tree watching it
all
as high on the
hill
the general stood
looking through his
dusty
binoculars.
he was senile
and drooled
little goblets out of
each side of his
mouth.

Los Angeles, Calif.,
summer 1938.
Saturday.
death had a little
black moustache
and he waited for
us
and many of us
went.

what will the neighbors think?

I think that was the question asked most of me
by my parents.
of course, I didn't really care what the
neighbors thought.
I felt sorry for the neighbors, those frightened
people peeking from behind their
curtains.
the whole neighborhood was watching
itself
and in the 1930s there wasn't much else to
watch.
except me coming in drunk late at
night.

"this is going to kill your mother,"
my father told me,
"and besides what will the
neighbors think?"

me, I thought I was doing very well.
one way or the other
I managed to get drunk
without having any
money at all.
a trick that would stand me in good
stead
later in my life.

to make things worse for my poor
parents
I began to write letters to the
editor of one of the large
newspapers,
most of which were published
and all of which
backed unpopular causes.

"what will the neighbors think?"

my parents asked
me.

but the letters brought interesting
results—hate letters, including
death threats through the
mails.
it also brought me into contact
with some weird
people who believed that I
meant what I had written in
those letters.

there were secret meetings
in cellars and attics,
there were guns, pacts,
plans,
speeches.
those were also
places where I scrounged up
free drinks.
most of these meetings
were attended by right-wingers,
young guys between the ages
of 17 and 23.
"we don't want blacks fucking
our women!
they must die!"
unfortunately
I wasn't fucking any
women myself.
all the meetings began by standing
and saluting the
flag
which I considered pretty
damned
juvenile.
but most of these young men
were from well-to-do
families

and I drank with some of
them afterwards.
I drank as much as I could
as they ranted
on.
I never said anything
but they didn't seem to mind.
they remembered the letters
and had no idea that they
were false.
not that I was a decent
human being
but I wasn't aligned
with any group or
ideology.
actually the whole idea of
life and people
repulsed me
but it was easier to
scrounge drinks off the
right-wingers
than off old women
in the bars.

"I don't believe that you
are a son of mine,"
my father told me.

"what will the neighbors
think?" my mother
asked.

poor damned patriotic
deluded fools.

after they threw me out
of the house
I gave up
the meetings
and went and lived by myself in a

plywood shack on
Bunker Hill.

and my parents no longer
had to worry about
what the
neighbors thought.

full circle

Sanford liked to play dirty
tricks like piss in milk bottles,
burn the legs off of spiders, torture
cats, put water in gas tanks, etc.

he was full of dirty
tricks.

we grew up together.

when World War II arrived he went into the
air force.

"the flyboys get all the pussy," he
told me.

on his second mission over the English
Channel they
blasted his ass out of the
sky.

they never found him.

one more dirty trick in a dirty trick
world.

2

the streets were all I saw

a place in Philly

there's nothing like being young
and starving,
living in a roominghouse and
pretending to be a
writer
while other men are occupied
with their professions and
their possessions.
there's nothing like being
young and
starving,
listening to Brahms,
your belly sucked-in,
nary an ounce of
fat,
stretched out on the bed
in the dark,
smoking a rolled
cigarette
and working on the
last bottle of
wine,
the sheets of your
writing strewn across the
floor.
you have walked on and across
them,
your masterpieces, and
either
they'll be read in
hell,
or perhaps
gnawed at by the
curious
mice.
Brahms is the only
friend you have,
the only friend you

want,
him and the wine
bottle,
as you realize that
you will never
be a citizen of the
world,
and if you
live to be very
old
you still will never
be a citizen of the
world.
the wine and
Brahms mix well as
you watch the
lights
move across the
ceiling,
courtesy of
passing
automobiles. .
soon you'll sleep
and
tomorrow there
certainly
will be
more
masterpieces.

the *Kenyon Review* and other matters

it was good being young but I didn't know it, a starving
jackass, stubborn beyond reason, reading that
tower of practiced literary horror, the *Kenyon Review*.
somehow I admired their gamesmanship, their snobby word
play, their inbred docility.
I was lower class, depraved, a spectacle, a dissolute
slave
yet I was oddly charmed by their petty jousting, their
safe anger, their shield of learnedness;
to read this journal and others and then return to my small
room or the bars of night (most often that) to meet
another breed—club-fisted, bleary-eyed, cantankerous,
grubby, and joining them in their downward dance.
drink tempered our defeat, it warmed us, it heated us.
our only challenge was ourselves, no one would have
anything to do with us.
rallied and maddened by drink, I tested these in the
alleys, these bulls, these bears, these dumb bastards,
and they were good at war and I was not so bad.
it was a doing, a going on, nothing else.
our space was small and a bit unkind.

the next day to return to the library with a shut eye,
a swollen lip, skinned fingers, a wrist that hurt and
flamed like hell.

to turn more pages, to find them thinner and thinner, less
and less, like gossamer wings that would not hold
strong light, I was caught between nowhere and nowhere, I
sat at that library table caught between suicide and
acquiescence
I was no longer young; I was older than the centuries.

I closed the last book, the last magazine then.

I walked out of there.

the streets were all I saw.

I walked into
them.

big night on the town

drunk on the dark streets of some city,
it's night, you're lost, where's your
room?
you enter a bar to find yourself,
order scotch and water.
damned bar's sloppy wet, it soaks
one of your shirt
sleeves.
it's a clip joint—the scotch is weak.
you order a bottle of beer.
Madame Death walks up to you
wearing a dress.
she sits down, you buy her a
beer, she stinks of swamps, presses
a leg against you.
the bartender sneers.
you've got him worried, he doesn't
know if you're a cop, a killer, a
madman or an
idiot.
you ask for a vodka.
you pour the vodka into the top of
the beer bottle.
it's one a.m. in a dead cow world.
you ask her how much for head,
drink everything down, it tastes
like machine oil.

you leave Madame Death there.
you leave the sneering bartender
there.

you have remembered where
your room is.
the room with the full bottle of
wine on the dresser.
the room with the dance of the
roaches.

Perfection in the Stars
where love died

laughing.

total madness

all right, I know that you are tired of hearing
it
but how about this one last time?
all those tiny rooms in all those cities,
going from one city to another
from one cheap rented room to another
terrified and sickened of what people were.
it was the same any place and every place,
thousands and thousands of miles spent
looking out the window of a Greyhound bus,
listening to them talk, looking at them,
their heads, their ears, the way they walked.
these were strangers from somewhere else,
lifeless parallel perpendiculars,
they drove the blade through my gut,
even the lovely girls,
with guile of eye, with the lilt and magic of
their bodies
where only a down payment on a
mirage,
life's cheap trick.

I went from room to room
from city to city,
hiding, looking, waiting ...
for what?
for nothing but the
irresponsible and negative
desire
to at least
not be like
them.

I loved those old rooms,
the worn rugs,
the walk down the hall
to the bathroom,
even the rats and the

mice and the roaches
were comrades...

and along the way
somehow I discovered
the classical composers.

I had an old record player.
and rather than eat
I used what funds I had
for cheap wine and
record albums.
and I rolled cigarettes,
smoked, drank,
listened to the music
in the dark.
I remember one particular
night
when Wagner really
lifted the ceiling off
my room
I got up
out of bed
joy-stricken,
I stood there and lifted
both arms toward the
ceiling
and I caught sight of
myself in the dresser
mirror
and there was nothing left
of me,
a skeleton of a man,
down from 200 pounds to
130,
with sunken
cheeks.
I saw this death skull
looking at me
and it was so

ridiculous and so lovely
that I started to laugh
and the thing in the mirror
laughed back
and it got
funnier and funnier
as I lifted my arms
higher toward the
ceiling.

and along with those old
rooms,
I was lucky,
I had gentle old landladies,
with pictures of
Christ on the stairways,
but they were always nice
in spite of that.

"Mr. Chinaski, your rent is
overdue, are you all
right?"

"oh, yes, thank you."

"I hear your music playing,
night and day,
you sit in your room night
and day with the shades
pulled down …
are you all right?"

"I'm a writer."

"a writer?"

"yes, I just sent something
to the *New Yorker*
I'm sure I'll be hearing from
them any day now."

somehow if you told them
you were a writer
they would put up with all
sorts of
excuses,
especially if you were
in your early
twenties.
(later on, it was a hard
sell
as I was to
find out.)

but I loved those
small rooms in all of
those cities with all
of those landladies
and Brahms
and Sibelius
and Shostakovich
and Ives
and Sir Edward Elgar
and the Chopin Etudes
and Borodin
Beethoven
Hayden
Handel
Moussorgsky,
etc.

now, somehow, after
decades of
those rooms
and half-assed barren
jobs
and after tossing out
literally 40 or 50
pounds of rejected
manuscripts
I still return to a

small room,
here,
to recount to you
once more
the wonder of
my madness
then.

the difference now
being
that while my writing hasn't
changed that much,
my luck
has.

and
it was in those rooms
in the half light of
some 4 a.m.
a shrunken man on the
shelf of nowhere
was young enough to
then
remain young
forever.

rooms of
glory.

on the bum

moving from city to city
I always had two pairs of
shoes,
my looking-for-work
shoes and my working
shoes.

my work shoes were
heavy and black
and stiff.
sometimes when I
first put them on
they were very
painful,
the toe
hardened and
twisted
but I'd get them
on
on a hangover
morning,
thinking, well,
here we go
again
working for
miserable wages
and expected to
be grateful
for that
(having been chosen
from a score of
applicants).
it was probably my
ugly and
honest
face.

putting on

those shoes
again
was always
another hard
beginning.

I
imagined myself
somehow
escaping
it all.
making it at the
gaming table
or in the
ring
or in the bed
of some rich
lady.

maybe I got
that notion from
living too long in
Los Angeles,
a place far too
close to
Hollywood.

but going down
those roominghouse
steps
with each new
beginning,
the stiff shoes
murdering my
feet,
stepping out into
the early
sun,
the sidewalk
there,

the city
there
and I was just one
more
common laborer,
one more
common
man,
the universe
sliding through
my head
and out my
ears,
the timecard waiting
to check me in
and out,
and afterwards
something to
drink and the
ladies from
hell.

work shoes
work shoes
work shoes
and me
inside of
them with
all the lights
turned
out.

society should realize...

you consult psychiatrists and philosophers
when things aren't going well
and whores when they are.
the whores are there for young boys and old
men; to the young boys they say,
"don't be frightened, honey, here I'll put it
in for you."
and for the old guys
they put on an act
like you're really hooking it home.
society should realize the value of the
whore—I mean, those girls who really enjoy their
work—those who make it almost an
art form.

I'm thinking of the time
in a Mexican whorehouse
this gal with her little bowl and her rag
washing my dick,
and it got hard and she laughed and I
laughed and she
kissed it, gently and slowly, then she walked over and
spread out
on the bed
and I got on and we worked easily, no effort, no
tension, and some guy beat on the door and·
yelled,
"Hey! what the hell's going on in there?
Hurry it up!"
but it was like a Mahler symphony—you just don't
rush
it.

when I finished and she came back, there was
the bowl and the rag again
and we both laughed; then she kissed it
gently and
slowly, and I got up and put my clothes back on and

walked out—
"Jesus, buddy, what the hell were ya doin' in
there?"
"Fuckin'," I told the gentleman
and walked down the hall and down the steps and stood
outside in the road and lit one of those
sweet Mexican cigarettes in the moonlight.
liberated and human again
for a mere $3, I
loved the night, Mexico and
myself.

madman

while
being
checked into the L.A. City jail (I
was still a bit drunk)
there was a crowd of prisoners waiting and
nobody noticed me smoking a cigarette
until some ash dropped off the end
then a cop screamed at me about how
"we kept this fucking place CLEAN!"
"oh," I said, and then the cop said,
"wise fucker, huh?...O.K., now you
get it!"
and he pushed me into a back room and
locked the door behind
me.
there behind a thick yellow floor-to-ceiling
wire screen was this total
madman
he saw me and screamed
ran violently toward me
smashed into the wire screen
bounced back
rushed the wire again
grabbing it
shaking it
wanting to get through it
trying to get at me
trying to kill me

it was frightening
but I was drunk
found another cigarette
lit it trembling
pushed it through the wire
expecting to get my hand ripped
off
he took the smoke
put it to his lips

inhaled
exhaled

I lit up
also
and we stood there together
smoking.

that's the way the cop
found us
when he opened the door
behind
me.

"son of a bitch," he said, "that's
beautiful, I wish I could let
you go for that."

"I wish you could too,"
I told him.

"come on," he
said.

as we walked out the door
the madman grabbed the wire again and
screamed
screamed
screamed
he rattled and banged the
wire
that thick wire
with the yellow paint flaking off
revealing the
pale grey paint
underneath.

nazi

suicide
in a
wino hotel

turn him on his
back

find the front
of him

chest
arms

sailing ships
snakes
girls

and even such
words as
love
Annie, words such as
Mother

and the secret tattoo
on the neck
that only jailbirds
know

he's picked cotton
rode the freights
worked the track gangs
maybe killed somebody

suicide in a
wino hotel:
now he's killed
somebody

turn him on his
back

find the front
of him

tears of the mountains
prints of the lonely fox

God's mark
like a swastika

16 Jap machine gun bullets

Norman
Jimmy
Max killed in World War II
while I hid in old roominghouses
in Philadelphia and San
Francisco
listening to
Mozart and Bach.

others fared differently:
with George it was a bad
liver. Dale died of misled
ambition. Nick went the common hard way of
cancer.
Harry of a
wife and 5 beautiful children.

Jimmy had it right—
trying to bring that bomber back to
England with the motors shot
out. Norman had it
right—
taking 3 hours to die from
16 Jap machine gun bullets.

now we've all got it quite right—
sitting around reading the
comic strips
drinking warm wine and
rolling smokes.
at 6 in the evening we charm our blood and
our manner
as we walk our faces through the
spiderwebs.

we've got it right
we've got it right—
the raven and the waves

the tired sunsets and the tired
people—
it takes a lifetime to die and
no time at
all.

bar stool

each day and each night were
about the same.
the bartender let me in at
5 a.m.
I had to listen to his stories
as he mopped the place up
and got things
ready
but the drinks were free
until 7 a.m. when the bar
opened.

the 7 a.m. crowd was a
good one,
I could usually work them
for some drinks
but by 8:15 a.m. there were
few patrons left.
I had to nurse my drinks
and wait.

I used the few coins I had
to keep the drinks slowly
arriving.
the painful time came
when I ran out of
coin.
the trick was to never
empty your glass.
it was a rule: as long as
you had something in
your glass you
stayed.

sometimes the time
really bludgeoned
me
and my damned

tongue was hanging
out too.

at noon a few
more would drift in,
they all knew
me.
I put on a good
late night
show—
wild sentences of
gibberish,
fist fights,
even a few
profound
statements,
and the times
I had money
I bought for
everybody.
I was the nut.
the good guy.
the bad
guy.
but in the daylight
hours I had
no zip.
those were the
hard hours.
I had to milk
those drab suckers
for
drinks.
one way or the other
I got them,
ran errands,
got a little
coin.

as the afternoon

went toward
evening
things began to
get better,
I got drunker,
more inventive,
more interesting,
it got into party
time,
good luck
time.

and the nights
were great.
drinks arrived
before me
and I had no
idea where they
had
come
from.

sometimes the
nights and the days
got mixed up.
I seemed to be
sitting in daylight
and then it was
dark all at once,
or it worked the
other way around,
it was dark
and in the next
moment
it was daylight.

I once asked the
bartender, "hey,
Jim, did you notice
that it was dark

and now the sun
is shining!
isn't that strange?"

"no," he answered,
"you went to your
room and then came
back again."

at times I resented
my role.
the patrons were
hardly intellectual,
there was a lifeless
and satisfied deadness
about them
and yet I had to
depend upon their
whims.
I was on
that bar stool for
3 years from 5 a.m.
to 2 a.m.
I must have slept
while I drank.
I believe that I was
trying to kill myself
with drink and
back alley
brawls
but it wasn't
working.
my greatest problem
were my toenails
which I never
cut
and which pained
me in my
shoes.
but eventually

they broke off
or the whole
nail would fall
off
leaving that
tender flesh
plus
a few split
lips,
mangled fingers,
lumps on the
knee
from falling,
and that was the
extent of
it.

I was evicted from
room after room
but always managed
to find
another.

it was as good a
life as I could
eke out.

I was avoiding
becoming ensnared
in a common
manner of
living.
I truly believed
that this was
important to me
when everything
else was
not.

and the one

stool was
mine.

the one down
at the end of
the
bar.

it was all that
I owned.
it was all that
I needed.

there was no
other man
I preferred to be
or no
other way that
I preferred.

I was at the
peak of my
courage,
sitting there
waiting for
that next
drink.
do you see
what I
mean?

the mirror game

Peter was a freak, Peter was fat, Peter
was dumb, Peter was clumsy, Peter stuttered
and Peter stumbled and the girls giggled at
Peter and the boys taunted him, and Peter
was often kept after school and Peter's glasses
always fell off and his shoe-
laces were untied and his shirttail hung
out and his clothing was unlike anything
we'd ever seen and Peter always sat
in a back seat in class with snot running
from his nose.

that was then. that was grammar school and
junior high, and time went
on and
now
Peter never drives his expensive car more than
one year and he always has a new and
beautiful girlfriend and he no longer wears
glasses and he has thinned down, looks al-
most handsome but certainly assured, he
has a home in Mexico and a home in Holly-
wood.
Peter deals in art work and the stock
market, he speaks three languages, has a
yacht and a private plane and he also
sometimes produces movies.

those who knew him then don't know him
now.
something
happened, what the hell
was it?

and most of the golden boys of yore
who are still around now
are misshapen, beaten, inglorious,
idiotic, homeless, senile or

dying.

it seldom works the way we think it
works.
in fact, it never
does.

liar, liar, pants on fire!

bunch of guys sitting there drinking and Louie
started in, said he was in this bedroom
working out when the woman under him said,
"It's my husband! I hear his key in the front
door!"
Louie jumped up, there was only one way
out, through the bathroom window, it was
two floors up but he went for it anyhow,
leaving his pants, his shirt, shoes, everything there,
he climbed out the window, ass-naked, and
let himself down by the drainpipe.
three quarters of the way down he fell to the
ground, got up with a sprained and twisted
ankle and hobbled to his car
which was parked in back and drove off
with a roar, away into the night totally
naked but still alive!

the guys laughed, "Man, Louie, you got
away with it!"

the way I saw it, Louie couldn't have
started his car without his
pants with the keys in them.
I knew that I could expose him, but
what was the good?

another fellow with a bullshit
story while I was thinking up one of my
own.

the inspection

it was a small dusty town in east Texas
full of wild turkeys.
I had just married the
daughter
and they had come to her
house to see who I
was.
all the relatives and the
devil knows
who else.

now it was over
and I was sitting on the
edge of the bed
sucking on a beer
bottle
and my wife stood
there.

"they liked you,"
she said.

"yeah?"

"they expected some city
boy, not
you."

"ah?"

"you drank more
whiskey than any of
them, even Uncle
Paul, and you
didn't even
blink."

"it was good

whiskey."

"you're accepted," said my
wife. "they won't
bother us."

"are they supposed
to?"

"they ran off my
last one..."

"your last one?
wait a minute
here..."

"we were engaged."

"anybody I know?"

she laughed.

"also, when they used
the word 'nigger' you
didn't protest."

"I thought they were
talking to me.
hell, baby, I'm a
nigger."

I walked to the
kitchen and got
another beer.
all the whiskey
was gone.

when I got back
she was standing
there

smiling.

"but you know,"
she said, "what
made the
biggest hit?"

"no, tell me…"

"it was when you walked
out wearing those filthy
blue jeans!"

"yeah?"

"oh, yes!
they won't chase you off
now!"

I had passed
muster.

the parade could
begin.

somewhere in Texas

sitting in a big ranch house with a grandmother
and a grandfather (not mine) and the grandmother
tells me she has "terrible migraines" and doesn't
know what to do.
I know she has one then and the reason is
that I am sitting in her house.
the grandfather asks me if I want a drink and I tell
him yes and he pours me a whiskey and
water
and my wife walks out and says, "don't start him
too early, it leads to trouble."
I slam the drink down, look at the grandfather, ask,
"how about another just like that last one?"
my wife walks away.
the afternoon winds down as I sit drinking with gramps
and then gramps falls asleep in his chair and I help
myself to more.
I sit with the setting sun in my eyes and it feels
good.
after a while I walk into the yard and there's an
Indian.
I sit on the ground and watch him build a
chicken coop.
after a while I ask him, "want a drink?"
he says no.
a no-fun guy.
I walk back into the house.
grandpop is still asleep.
grandma still has her migraine.
I walk through the house.
I walk back to the bedroom.
my wife is standing there.
"you son-of-a-bitch," she says.
"of course," I say.
I flop down on the bed, look up at the
ceiling.
among the cracks I make out an angel, a goat and a
lion.

my wife walks out of the room.
I wonder what they pay the Indian.
not much: room, board, a pot to piss
in.
I decide to sleep.
maybe later that night things would look
better.

city boy

I stopped in Wyoming to drink in a bar
in Cheyenne.
maybe I looked Los Angeles.
one guy at the bar asked another,
"you wearin' boots?"
and the other guy answered,
"yeah, I'm wearin' boots."
I was sitting between them and
they talked around me.
"I don't think you're wearin' boots,"
the first guy said.
"well, I am," the other guy answered.
then it got quiet and they just looked at
each other.

I took a hit of my beer bottle,
set it down.

"nobody asked me," I said, "but
I'm going to tell you anyhow.
I've never worn boots and I hope that I
go to my grave never wearing
boots."

"maybe that can be arranged,"
said the first guy.

"that's possible," I said, "but who's
going to arrange it?"

"oh, that won't be any problem,"
said the first guy.

"it's at least going to cause some kind
of a problem, don't you think?" I said.

"no, not much."

"well, maybe not, but I am kind of
curious. who's going to do the
arranging? you?"

"maybe."

"you're going to let me wonder,
huh?"

"yep."

"well, while I'm wondering, I think I'll
have a drink of whiskey.
hey, bartender!"

this big guy came ambling down.

"yeah?"

"will you please pour me a shot of
whiskey to wonder over?"

he ambled off to get it.

it got quiet in there.

my whiskey came ambling back.

I slammed it down.

"I kind of like this town," I said, "I think
I'll stay awhile."

"maybe," said the guy who had been
doing all the talking.

"you're full of maybies," I said.
"How'd you get that way?"

"maybe I'm not going to tell

you."

then it was quiet again, there were
6 or 7 guys in that
bar.

I took a hit of my beer.

then I looked at the other guy
sitting next to me.

"you're not wearing boots,"
I told him.

"didn't say I was."

then it got very quiet.
everybody just sat there.

it stayed quiet.

"bartender," I said finally, "a round of drinks
for everybody."

they were all drinking beer.

the bartender went about setting up
new beers.
then he was finished.

I put some bills on the bar.
the bartender came down and
took all of them.

he walked down to the register,
hit it and dropped my money
into it.
then he took a rag and mopped
the bar.

I got up and walked to the
door.
then I turned and looked.

the bartender was still mopping
the bar.
the other guys just sat
looking straight ahead.

I turned and walked out
of the bar.

nobody said
goodbye.

the strange morning outside the bar

it had never happened before and one doesn't
know how such things can
happen.

it was about 11 a.m. and I had stopped
outside for some air.
Danny walked up and I started talking
to Danny.
then Harry walked up and joined us
on the corner.

then I noticed two other men
stop and begin talking
to each other a few feet away.

"let's go in for a drink," I said to
Danny and Harry.

"no, it's nice out here," said Danny,
"let's gab awhile."

so we did.

then I noticed some more men
arrive.
some were talking, others
just stood there.

it happened slowly.

more and more men arrived
at the corner.

it was getting crowded.

it was getting almost
humorous.

there was something
strange in the air,
you could feel it.

there were many voices
now.
and more men arrived.
I don't know where they
came from.

they stood around
talking,
laughing,
and smoking
cigarettes.

Jim the bartender stuck
his head out the door
and asked,
"hey, what the hell's
going on out here?"

somebody laughed.

Jim went back inside to
the empty bar.

I began to feel very
strange about it all,
as if the world had
decided to change,
all at once.

there was a feeling of
joy and gamble in
the air.
I believe that everybody
felt it.

it was a powerful energy

let loose and working
upon itself.

then Jack the cop
walked up.
"hey, you guys,
break it up!
what the hell is all
this?"

we all knew Jack,
we drank with him
at night.

soon Jack was standing there
talking and listening
to the others.

Danny grinned, "Jesus,
this is very strange."

"I like it," I said.

the whole corner was
crowded with
humanity
finally cut loose and
free,
laughing.

cars slowed down and the
drivers looked out
wondering what was
happening.
we didn't
know.

finally I said,
"I can't stand this
anymore, I'm going in

for a drink."

Danny and Harry
followed me
in.

soon a few others
followed.

"lot of guys out there,"
said the bartender.

"yeah," said Harry, "but
where are the
women?"

"the women don't
want anything to do
with bums like us,"
said Danny.

we each had a couple
of drinks.
it took maybe 15 or
20 minutes.

then I went to the
door and looked
out.
everybody was
gone.

I came back and
sat down.

"wonder where they
went?"

"strangest morning of
my life," said

Danny.

"yeah," said
Harry.

we sat there thinking
about it.
then Danny started
talking about how his
parents were going to
throw him out for
too much
drinking.

Jim the bartender
stood there polishing
glasses
and things were back
to normal,
even to wondering
who was going to
buy the next
round.

a $15 boy and a $1500 casket

We can get you a nice boy with
soprano voice to sing behind a purple
curtain for just
$15, and I say
all right
all right, and my uncle says,
men like mahogany, you ought to get him the
mahogany, and I think,
doesn't he realize that this man is dead?
all right, I say.
the mahogany is $1500.

a day or so later
outside the parlor
getting a coffee
I meet my father's best friend
who tells me all his
troubles, and I say,
look, Bert, hate to interrupt you, but
I think I'm late, and
I run across the street
with Bert behind me,
and sure, they were waiting for me,
and I sat down and they
began.

they had the lid open on the coffin
and my $15 boy began to
sing, but I'd always hated my father,
still did, and then they lined up
to walk past his
coffin. I was the last, being the
son.

I should spit on his phoney face,
I thought, but then his girlfriend
who was right ahead of me
started weeping, moaning and

lifted that dead head up out of the coffin
and started kissing that dead head,
those dead lips.

well, the old boy had finally turned out to be
a lady's man.

I really didn't care
but I reached over and pulled the heads apart,
the dead one and the living one,
pushed her off, watched the old man's head
flop back into the casket,
not so nice now,
the rouge and powder smeared,
the cotton in the jaws pushed around,
lines and age showing, I knew I'd soon be dead too
but what a hell of a way to do it,
a $15 boy and a $1500 casket
when everybody knew what a son-of-a-bitch he
had been,
and when I walked down the steps
there she was
after kissing the dead head of that son-of-a-bitch,
she grabbed me, kissed me, sobbing
she tongued me
managing to say,
you look just like him, and
that made me mad
and I pushed her off
walked down the steps
drove to Santa Anita
met a high yellow
won $185
went to her place
had steak salad whiskey beer talk
went to bed together
and did it
several times

that was some years ago

but now every time I drive past that street
where she lived—
Irolo Street—

I think, yes the kissing of the dead head
the sleeping with the high yellow
the good day at the track
mahogany uncles be damned,
you worked with what was
left and forgot everything
else, which is the kindest way for
all of us.

rosary

my father was a man full of small
sayings:

"early to bed and early to
rise..."

"a fool and his money ..."

"you made your bed now lie in
it ..."

"a penny saved is..."

"do as I say, not as I have
done..."

"if you don't succeed, suck
eggs..."

there were others but I have
forgotten them.
how he would toll them off,
endlessly!

when he died I went to look at
him in his casket.
everybody talked about how good
he looked, "*peaceful!* look at him,
how *peaceful!* they've fixed him up
real nice!"

I just looked at him
almost expecting him to pop off
one of his sayings:

"a dead ass is better than no
ass at all ..."

"don't you wonder where I'm chasing
daffodils now?"

but nothing happened so I walked
away
followed by uncle
who said, "hey, Henry, let's
go get something to eat!"

"I know just the place," I said.
"follow
me…"

I could almost hear him saying
from the casket:

"the way to a man's heart is
through his
stomach…"

the smirking dark

when I buried my father, death stood there
and afterwards I got into my old car and drove
to the racetrack
and I stood there and watched the numbers flash
on the toteboard
and death still stood there
looking at all the people.
and I said, "you killed Dostoevsky."
he didn't answer, he just stood there.
I made a bet and lost, went to the men's room.
death followed me, stood there watching the men
at the urinals.
"you son-of-a-bitch," I said, "you made Van Gogh
blow himself away."
he didn't answer me.
then he followed me out.
he walked away, following a young girl in a red
dress.
I went and got a coffee, spilled some of it over
my fingers, it was hot.
I found a seat and thought about the next
race.
then death was back.
he was sitting next to me disguised as an old
guy with a scraggly white beard.
"who do you like in the next race?" he asked.
"you son-of-a-bitch," I said, "get away from
me!"
"what the hell's wrong with you?"
he asked.
"I told you, get the fuck away from
me!"
he got up and moved
off.

I didn't see him anymore at the
track.
after the last race

I took the freeway on in.

after 3 miles traffic began to
slow down.
I stayed in the left lane and
rode it out.

then I saw it,
on the other side of the freeway
fence—
a pile-up, bad,
one car on its roof,
another crushed on the freeway
fence,
a flame was beginning to flicker under
the hood, red lights came flashing
and inside my gut
something sucked and banged.

I drove past.
I drove on.

I parked outside my place,
got out, went in.
I opened the door.
there was nobody there.

then I saw the teddy bear.
it was pushed face-down into the pillow
on the bed.

I walked quickly to the stocking
drawer where the money was
kept.
my shipping clerk money.

only half of it was gone.

nice, I thought.

real class, you bitch.

then the door opened and death
walked in.

"care for a drink?" I asked
him.

he didn't answer.

I walked to the kitchen to see
if there was one.

the centuries flashed
by.

as he stood
waiting.

two crazies

we were the only two whites in the
factory.
he was real crazy, Max,
cocked neck, gangly thin arms, never
looked straight at anybody, well, he did
but it was only a quick glance from
atop a twisted neck and his eyes
were small and ugly and
dim, and he always wore brown:
brown shoes, brown shirt, brown
pants, brown socks
and his movements were
ungainly.
nobody ever spoke to him.
I was the other crazy
but the other workers didn't know
it.
I had a mean mouth, was good
with the quips and it gained me
some respect
but I was as out of it as
Max was.
I knew exactly how Max felt
and I think he knew how I felt
but it was a secret between
us.
we never spoke.
months went by and we never
spoke.
then one afternoon he spoke.
he turned and looked at me
and said, "you don't have any
guts."

at lunch time we squared off
in the alley behind the shop.
Max rushed me, winging punches
but they were butterfly

punches.
I took him easy, bloodied his
nose right away, then just
started leveling off.
it was like fighting a girl.
he didn't have
it.
the fellows pulled me
away.
we went back in
and Max went to the
washroom to clean
himself up.

nothing happened between
Max and myself
after that.
a month went by
and one day Max didn't
show up
and we never saw him
again.

a week or so later
I was fired.

and both the crazy whites
were gone.

Max had been
right:
I didn't have any guts.
I was shacked with a woman
ten years older
and I was
pussy-whipped
and lost in my own dream.
and if that ain't crazy,
I'd rather
be.

a note on the masses

private hells made public
often puzzle the readers:
they wonder how this one
or that one
can endure and
continue.
well, there's a secret:
don't expect too
much of Humanity,
they have been
practicing hatred
for centuries,
it's passed down
refined and
perfected,
oh, they have become
very good at that—
their hatreds blossom
with ever more frequent
regularity.
our public hell creates a
private hell and
there is no hell
except on
earth.
once you accept
this premise
you will be free to
exist
on your own terms
and you will never
know loneliness
and death will be as
nothing.
consider yourself
blessed in the
dark.

3

the singing of fools
and the volcano laughing

Lord Byron

he looked like Lord Byron
(or he said he did)
I don't know what Byron
looked like
I couldn't even read
him,
but Albert was tall,
fairly well-built
and he had bright
yellow hair,
a whole mane of it,
and his eyes were a
fierce blue
and he had a well-
modulated English
accent
and dozens of
women.
he professed to be
a writer
but I never saw
any of it.
I have no idea
where his income
came
from.
but he always lived
in well-furnished
apartments
with some young
lady of
education.
and as I saw him
on and off
through the years,
he became older
but his ladies
remained

the same
age: 22, 23,
24.

if there is a point
to all this
(and there may
not be) well, it was
that Albert loved
to drink
and I was perhaps
the best
drinker he knew
and he would
invite me over
to imbibe with
him.

it may have been
the contrast—
I was ugly and
crass, I'm sure
I made him look
all the better
to his ladies.

so I would crank
up the old car
and drive over for
the free
booze.

it was always about
the same:
Lord Byron couldn't
hold his drink,
kept running to the
bathroom to puke,
even though I was
outdrinking him

3 to one.

at
puking time,
I would make a
play for his
lady.

"come on, babe,
let's work in a
quicky while he vomits his
guts out on the
tiles and in the
toilet."

"you are
disgusting!"

"thank you,
mam."

then Albert would
exit pale from the
bathroom,
go to the bookcase,
pull out the work
of Keats or Shelley,
read us
one.
or he would go to
his sound system
and gift us with a
bit of
Vivaldi.

Lord Byron and I were
direct opposites:
he too sensitive to
live in the world
and I too thick to

understand his
pain.

but I was poor and
the drinks were
free
and I got to look up
the finely crossed legs
of his numerous
ladies,
so it was a fair
trade.

until true to his
delicate calling
he suicided one hangover
morning
after finding
a purse full of
pills
belonging to one
of his ladies
and I had to find another
poet to
milk free drinks
outa.

the weak

are always proclaiming that
they are now going to concentrate
on their *work*, which is usually
painting or writing.
it is known, of course, that they have
talent, they simply haven't...well...
they haven't truly been given a
chance.
there were matters that got
in the way: bad affairs, children,
jobs, illness, etc.
but now, that's all put aside, they
proclaim.
they are going to concentrate
on their work
they are finally going to do it
now.
they have the talent.
now the world will see.
oh yes, it's going to happen.

the proclaimers are everywhere.
they are always getting
ready.
they seldom begin.
and when they do
they quit easily.
it's all a whim with
them.
they want fame.
they want it quickly
but they really have no urge
to do their work
except for fame
and to proclaim,
proclaim,
proclaim.

a tough time

"I was a student of philosophy,"
said the guy at the end of the bar.
"good," said a guy at the middle
of the bar.
"how'd you like to come down
here and lick my balls?"

it was a hot night and the
air conditioner had broken
down.

I wasn't feeling good myself.
some university mag had
returned 15 of my poems with
a scrawled note:
"we don't read in the
summer ..."

it was something about the
note, the handwriting, the
lazy effrontery of it.

and at the track, on my big
bet of the day
the horse had thrown the
jock coming out of the
gate.
also, my left front tire had
a slow leak
and my wife had
PMS
again.

"I don't think you have any
balls," said the guy at the
end of the bar to the guy
at the middle of the
bar.

"oh yeah?" said the guy
accused of not having
any.

"yeah," said the accuser.

life was in a very stupid phase
for me.
I mean, I wasn't in a hospital,
I wasn't having a tooth
pulled,
my taxes were paid and
my shoelaces were
tied
but I felt rubbed
against by nasty
forces.
nothing beautiful,
unusual or even decent
had happened to me
for weeks.
my fault?
maybe.

"you can suck my ass,"
said the guy accused of
not having any balls.

"I can see you have an
ass," said the student of
philosophy, "because
I can see it sitting up
where your head
should be."

"listen, fellow," came the
response, "if you're looking
for a knuckle sandwich
you came to the right
guy."

they are not reading in
the summer, I thought,
what are they doing,
lolling in a hammock
lofting farts into a
gentle breeze?
free drinks for Dylan
Thomas and a
scurrilous note for
me.

"you and whose army
is going to handle
me?"
said the guy at the
end of the bar.

"I'm the army!
me!"

"that right?
you better get the
navy too, man!"

you ever read the
poems in those
university mags?
tiny dribblings of
unreality,
boring probes
into the
nonsensical.

I finished my drink,
got up to walk
out.

"I studied under
Prof. Harris
at City College,"

the guy at the end
of the bar
repeated.

"sure you did,"
said the guy at
the middle of the
bar,
"you were under
him,
face down,
on the springs!"

I stepped out into
the night just in time
to see a car hit a woman
crossing the street.
she flipped up
on the hood
on her back.
stayed there.
the guy jumped out of
the car and screamed,
"JESUS CHRIST!"

suddenly there were
125 people in the
street.

I turned and walked
away from it.
there was nothing I
could do.

when I got to my car
the left front tire was
flat.
I got in and sat
there.
the fog was rolling

in.
I turned on the
ignition
and clicked the
radio on.
it had been a
crappy
summer.

some luck, somehow

I was already an old man
working there,
nearing 50,
had been there eleven
years
working the night shift,
this young guy came
along,
blond, swift, full of
energy.
he told me at a coffee
break one
night:
"I'm only going to be
here a year, I'm working
on my novel."

twenty years later
I heard he's still there,
and worse, that he's
given up
writing.

some of those jocks
deserve the dull
jobs
they hate.

so many of those
jobs are held
by
first time
novelists.
I was one of
them
but somehow I knew
that the gods were
watching

so I never told
anybody.

and still
to this day
there are billions
of people
who don't know!

art class

of course, it wasn't my idea.
to me, Art is a fairly dirty word used by a large number
of people hiding behind walls of themselves;
I'm afraid I'm a shit and I prefer it that
way. that's all right
because I play my small game
and let alone what should be
let alone.

but the mother suggested our daughter
attend Saturday art class
and what's a drunk and a gambler and an unemployed man
to say? I pay a bit of child support, it's worth it,
she's a good little rag of a girl and we laugh a lot.
but the mother believes in Art,
she runs with a whole mad gang like that—
they chew on Art like vultures, suckerfish,
the blathering soul of Wilde, well, never mind,

don't let me get into that, o.k.?

the first one or 2 times were all right
I was just a strange man
standing there.

then later when the mothers saw
how my child ran to me with such delightful fury and
trust
I was almost accepted as if I
cared.

but as the weeks went on
the parents began to know each other,
speak to each other.

there was one perfectly terrible man,
a square something built of wood, he moved toward me
stiffly several times, smiling. I managed to walk off or lean over

the wall as if sick. he finally gave up.
and then there was one worse than any other,
strangely diseased beard, eyes always happy, wore purple and
red and yellow, very interested in life, always thrusting himself on
everybody, a very fine fellow.
meanwhile I had broken my small toe, right foot,
while drunk and so when he moved toward me
it was with much difficulty
that I had to walk away down the steps as if I had forgotten
my ham sandwich
or my collected works of Keats.

soon the parents began to understand
and they stood in their circles talking
and I stood alone in my circle
not talking.

there was one young teacher, female,
in room 6 who looked like she needed a good
lay
and since I am a very old and evil-looking man
I stared at her ass tits lips ears everything
whenever she came out of room
6. she hated me and that gave me some amusement
while I waited for my
daughter.

the last Saturday was the worst.
I arrived
hung over.

then, at noon, from room 3,
Barnsdall Park, they ran out
and I thought, fine, I'll get the girl
and we'll play Batman and Robin
eat ice cream and forget the Art con.

but Jesus, they all ran toward me—
the teacher, a rather blushing type, male,
probably a nice person, though, and all that,

but here they came
all running toward
me.

16 little girls between 5 and 9
and 12 little boys between 5 and 9,
and the Art teacher blushing
running
and they have 2 or 3 large plastic balloons
scrawled with peace signs and colorful
designs, and I can't get out of the
way. my little girl is in there somewhere,
and I think, Jesus Christ, how phoney, how sickening.
how sickening the nice people are
and
it's all Art-shit, the trick,
everybody loads their trick on somebody else
and then they let their helium-filled balloons fly
into the sky
and my little girl said,
"Hank, Hank, come here and watch!"
so I went there and watched
and the Art teacher said,
"What's going to happen to them?
Tell me, what's going to happen to them?"
and he blushed
and he was thinking of the 2 or 3
helium-filled balloons
with their peace signs
and I was thinking about the 16 little girls
between 5 and 9
and 12 little boys between 5 and 9,
and I took my kid's hand
and I limped down the long stairway with her
(I had re-smashed the toe) and she said,
thinking about the balloons, "it's kind of sad."
and I said, "Yes, it is," then we found my blue 1962
Comet. we got in together, it started,
and we turned left and drove down Hollywood Boulevard
past a carwash. "Look," she said, "all those men in those

125

orange overalls rubbing those cars with rags. why do
they do that?"

"that's so they can stay alive," I told
her.
"that's sad too," she said.

that's right, it was sad, it was their
Art, with very little blushing,
just work and wait and work and wait
as the sun is wasted
as they are wasted.

when we got to my place
she showed me her paintings and I said
"very nice, can I have this one?"

and she said, "sure."

I hung it on the wall.
it's looking at me now.
it's a girl's face done all in red
and the mouth is speaking. it says
"o.k.," then it says
"no."

that's Art—Batman, Robin or
Plato couldn't have said it any
better.

payoff

I was to give a poetry reading
at a Venice coffeehouse
but we got there early
so I told the woman,
let's walk down by the sea
and I can drink a beer,
so we walked down through the sand
and there were some men there fishing
and I faced the ocean
and had a good drink
and then I said,
let's go back and walk along the boardwalk
and we walked east
and then I noticed a man standing alone
with his back to the sea.
and he lifted a horn,
played a quiet and brief melody, and
stopped.
then he simply stood there
with his back to the sea.
I had another drink
and we walked on.
then, on the way back,
he was still there
and he lifted the horn again
and played the same
quiet, sad melody, finished,
and holding the horn down at his side,
he stood there.

it was hot in the coffeehouse
and I threw my stuff at them
and got away with
it, climbed down
and then we were back in the car
driving toward my
place. "you read well," she said.
"yeah," I said, "thanks."

but for me, the horn player had won the night,
and I felt the roll of bills in my pocket,
the payoff, and
I knew that night I had met a better man
and the better man had
won, and that was as it should
have been. but only the two of us
knew it.

ding-dong

he came over with a turban tied around his
head, and the long end of that turban
dangled down by his side
like a bell-cord.
it often got in his way
as he tried to light a cigarette
or lift his drink.

his girlfriend was dressed in a
fur outfit
that came down and covered her
feet.
her eyes were large and nice
and seemed always near
tears.
but she was
quiet.

he wasn't.

he jumped up often
spilling his drink on his
flowered shirt
he was six-feet-four and
worse than a bore.

it was at my place
and there were others
there.

I grabbed him by his belt and
pulled him to one side and
said, "what the fuck are you
on? I mean, buddy, you're
driving everybody *crazy*! do I
have to kick your *ass* just to
get a modicum of
silence?"

he just went on
talking.

I went back and sat down.
he followed and sat down
next to me.
he was a computer engineer.

he and the girl in the
fur outfit were going to
be married.
I knew I'd never go
to that wedding.

there was a fellow sitting on the floor
across from the coffee table
who told really
interesting and funny stories
but all any of us could hear was
the computer engineer.

after a while
we gave up and just
listened
although nobody could understand
much of what he was saying....

the computer engineer and his
girl
were friends of the lady
I lived with
and since my lady
liked to say that
I treated her friends
badly
I just sat there and drank
as the tall one
leaped up and sat down again
talking
and getting tangled in his

bell-cord.

I glanced over at the lady
I lived with.
she was smiling pleasantly
as he screamed his
nonsense.

and I thought, if I am being
tested I am failing again.
I can't find *anything*
interesting in any of
this

and I reached out and
yanked his
bell-cord....

still talking
his head
jerked
down
and he spilled his drink
on me

sat upright
and began again with
more vigor than
ever

only the head-jerk
seemed to clear his speech
patterns
and I finally began to understand what
he was saying.

he was telling the world
that
I was an
antisocial hunk of

despicable shit. that
brotherhood and sisterhood
would engulf my work and my
petty ways. that
every man was a poet and
every woman was too.

I poured him a new
drink.

he picked it up and
snouted it
down.

love is what mattered,
he went on,
and
furthermore ...

AFDC for you and me

these dogs, she said, are always sticking their
noses in my crotch, it's exasperating
I don't know what they
want.
she had on dark pink pantyhose
and had hands 50 years old and a face 40
but she was in her late
20s, early 30s,
one psychiatrist after another,
she was on
AFDC, just like the rest of us wanted to be.
we discussed how we had bad feelings when we
killed certain types of bugs,
but we decided it was all right to kill
spiders and cockroaches
and it was all right to eat fish and crabs
and lobsters,
also chickens didn't have any damned brains
but pigs were smarter than horses,
you couldn't eat pigs.
I'm a cocktail waitress, she said,
and I wear this mini-skirt but I sure get tired
of those men staring at my
crotch. I get so drunk
that I spill drinks on people,
and later on I sing,
not rock, that's dead,
I sing jazz …
will you marry me? I asked.
yes, she said.

then she and her boyfriend got into a kind of
argument and they left me there with the wine bottle and
I sat eating fried chicken
and listening to Shostakovich
until 5 a.m.
in the morning.

I know you

you with long hair, legs crossed high, sitting at the end of
the bar, you like a butcher knife against my throat
as the nightingale sings elsewhere while laughter
mingles with the roach's hiss.
I know you as
the piano player in the restaurant who plays badly,
his mouth a tiny cesspool and his eyes little wet rolls of
toilet paper.
you rode behind me on my bicycle as I pumped toward Venice as
a boy, I knew you were there, even in that brisk wind I smelled
your
breath.
I knew you in the love bed as you whispered lies of passion while
your
nails dug me into you.
I saw you adored by crowds in Spain while pigtail boys with
swords
colored the sun for your glory.
I saw you complete the circle of friend, enemy, celebrity and
stranger as the fox ran through the sun carrying its heart in its
mouth.
those madmen I fought in the back alleys of bars were
you.
you, yes, heard Plato's last words.
not too many mornings ago I found my old cat in the yard,
dry tongue stuck out awry as if it had never belonged, eyes tangled,
eyelids soft yet, I lifted her, daylight shining upon my
fingers and her fur, my ignorant existence roaring against the
hedges and the flowers.
I know you, you wait while the fountains gush and the scales
weigh,
you tiresome daughter-of-a-bitch, come on in, the door is
open.

bone palace ballet

as many interpretations of
Mozart's "Mass in C"
as fleas upon my favorite cat,
or as many garbagemen of verse
in a world full of flamingos.

this
tired
life
this dusty dream,
these April nights,
this thunder in a paper cup,
all the old ladies
alone in rooms
working crossword puzzles,
the dead dogs of forever
crushed with
lolling tongues,
the parched innards of
mountains
aching to
scream,
what is this grueling
nonsense?

is it
the worm crawling toward
no paradise?
the scissors in a closed
drawer?
young girls giggling and
lost in their flesh?
the night and then the
day or
the day and then the
night?
the hammer?
the saw?

the mirror which swings
open?

and what about
the dark streets of Dublin?
the last page of the book?
the green park bench alone?
the last necktie?
the last footstep
behind you?

this incomplete sob of darkness.
a wingless bird waiting.
a druid in the wasted light.
a drunk in the gutter.
the singing of fools
and the volcano laughing.

oh

in the bar
the beer bottle in somebody's
hand
has no chance.
outside there is the sound
of car tires in the
rain.
there is a flash of
lightning.
somebody
laughs.

what can you do?

there is always somebody to chop wood
for you,
to speak of
God,
there is always somebody to kill the
meat,
to unplug the toilet,
there is always somebody to bury
you,
there are always animals with
beautiful eyes,
and there are always those
like Stanley leaning toward me
and saying in a soft voice,
"do you know that at the end of
his career Saroyan had other
people writing his stuff and that he
gave them twenty-five
percent?"
this was supposed to make me
feel original,
feel good because I was a starving
writer and the rejects were arriving
in record numbers.
it didn't make me feel
good.

there is always somebody or something
to make
you feel worse.

there is always the dead dog on
the freeway.
there is always a fog full of
cutting
blades.

there is always Christ drunk in
the tavern with dirty
fingernails.

my friend, the parking lot attendant

—he's a dandy
—small moustache
—usually sucking on a cigar

he tends to lean into cars as he
transacts business

first time I met him, he said,
"hey! ya gonna make a
killin'?"

"maybe," I answered.

next meeting it was:
"hey, Ramrod! what's
happening?"

"very little," I told
him.

next time I had my girlfriend with me
and he just
grinned.

next time I was
alone.

"hey," he asked, "where's the young
chick?"

"I left her at home...."

"*Bullshit*! I'll bet she dumped
you!"

and the next time
he really leaned into the car:

"what's a guy like *you* doing driving a
BMW? I'll bet you inherited your
money, you didn't get this car with your
brains!"

"how'd you guess?" I
answered.

that was some weeks ago.
I haven't seen him lately.
fellow like that, chances are he just moved on
to better
things.

last will and testament

you stop agonizing for a while
thinking that maybe life's true
essence has risen to the
top (temporarily)
or that a minor decency,
a minor sensibility
has taken a gentle
hold.
but it's illusion, all
illusion:
the crap is still crap,
the old structure remains
firmly
in place,
you're going to have to
endure
the same hollow ghosts
of love,
the same cardboard
faces,
the same eyeless
eyes,
the old dark,
the same old dark,
the same knock
on the door
with nobody on the
other
side.
we are not without
joy,
we have what we
need here,
and my wish is simple
enough,
although it may
not be granted:
that the living dead

of this life
will not soon
die
and then follow,
after the graciousness
of death
hopefully rescues me
from the monstrous
weight of
this drizzling
suckerfish
nightmare.

12 minutes to post

as we stand there before the purple mountains
in our stupid clothing, we pause, look
about: nothing changes, it only congeals,
our lives crawl slowly, our companions depreciate
us.
then
we awaken a moment—
the animals are entering the track!
Quick's Sister, Perfect Raj, Vive Le Torch,
Miss Leuschner, Keepin' Peace, True To Be,
Lou's Good Morning.

now, it's good for us: the lightning flash
of hope, the laughter of the hidden gods.
we were never meant to be what we are or where
we are, we are looking for an escape, some music
from the sun, the girl we never found.
we are betting on the miracle again
there before the purple mountains
as the horses parade past
so much more beautiful than
our lives.

in the center of the action

you have to lay down like an animal
until it
charges, you
have to lay down
in the center of the action

lay down and wait until it charges then you
must get
up
face it get
it before it gets
you

the whole process is more
shy than
vulnerable so

lay down and wait sometimes it's
ten minutes sometimes it's years sometimes it
never arrives but you can't rush it push
it
there's no way to cheat or get a
jump on it you have to

lay down
lay down and wait like
an animal.

the fool

I sat in that cheap hotel room
waiting.
I sat drinking wine and
waiting.
I turned out the lights and
drank in the
dark.

the phone rang.
it was her.
"I'll be along in a little
while, Hank."
"when?"
"just a little while, wait
for me, don't
worry."

she hung up.
she was one of my first
women.
ten years older than
I.
the hotel was on 6th
street.

I sat in the dark
drinking the
wine.
soon the bottle was
empty.

I went out,
took the elevator down,
to get
another.

when I got back
I asked the desk clerk

if there had been any
messages.
he looked at me as if
I were crazy.

I took the elevator back
up.

I was about halfway
through the second
bottle when the phone
rang.
"Hank, it's me, I'll be
there real
soon."
she hung
up.

I sat in the dark and
finished the
bottle.
then I got out of
there and took the
elevator
down.

I walked half a
block
took a left
walked down to the
bar.

through the blinds
I could see her
sitting at the
bar.
she was smoking
drinking
talking to some
old guy in a

wrinkled grey
suit.

I walked down
to my car,
got in
and drove out
of there.

saw her somewhere a
couple of weeks
later and
she said,
"geez, Hank, what
happened?
I went up to that
room and there was
nobody
there!"

"no kidding?" I said,
"you mean you went there
and there was nobody
there?"

she knew it was
over.

she opened her purse
and looked down
into it,
fumbling
around.

looking for cigarettes,
a lighter
or her next
move.

the rock

I will not name this poet although his blood-red and dark
words impressed themselves upon me and still
do.
in mid-life he became and remained a complete
recluse.
he spoke to no one and was seen by very few.
his work and his life appeared to be as one.

it was not until after his death that I read his
Collected Letters and these
pandered to university powers and publishing
forces.
there was letter after letter of
beckoning and
posturing, of
obeisance and
compromise.

he hardly seemed the same man.
maybe he wasn't, I thought, maybe somebody else wrote those
letters for him
and then
they were published.

in reality, though, I knew that he had written
them.

how soon our idols fall
until
there are none
left.

ah

it will never end, there will be no
help, no mercy, no living thing,
it will all go on, uselessly, through
fabrication and old habits, it
will continue, a headless body
of life, walking old walks, doing
old tricks, dreaming old dreams,
it will be as alone as a mountain,
and despite billions of beings
there will not be one real being, there
will be everlasting waste and only
the animals will be real, they will have
the pureness of eye and the grace,
they will be the last, the simple,
pure, the ember, what it meant
truly, the wolf will have the heart
and the panther the lungs and
the eagle, the eyes, and the last
war will be one man sitting in a
chair, laughing at it
all.

room 106

came to town in the middle of the night
found a motel room
lit a cigarette
and looked at the black and white
tv,
a couple in the next room
arguing,
they sound drunk,
Southern,
I turn the tv off,
look through the blinds,
my car is still there,
I take my shoes and clothes off,
too tired to shower,
I manage to brush my teeth,
come back,
switch out the lights,
stretch out in the bed in the
dark,
I can hear them still
arguing,
it isn't a very interesting
argument,
I'm tired,
want to sleep
and soon they stop arguing
and I listen to the traffic
going by
but I can't sleep,
somehow I think of myself as
a dead man
on that bed,
I'm dead, the maid will
find me when she comes
to change the sheets and
towels.
upon seeing me
she will make a small

frightened sound,
close the door
and run off
somewhere.

that scene seems appealing
to me,
quite,
I yawn, stretch, turn on my
right side,
see the red
NO VACANCY sign through
the blinds
and just like that I
am
asleep.

in other words

the Egyptians loved the cat
were often entombed with it
instead of with the women
and never with the dog

but now
here
good people with
good eyes
are very few

yet fine cats
with great style
lounge about
in the alleys of
the universe.

about
our argument tonight
whatever it was
about
and
no matter
how unhappy
it made us
feel

remember that
there is a
cat
somewhere
adjusting to the
space of itself
with a delightful
grace

in other words
magic persists

without us
no matter what
we may try to do
to spoil it.

the horseplayer

how strange it is on
a hot summer
night
to come back in
and go over your figures
trying to piece together the action
at the track,
sitting in your undershirt,
sucking on a cold beer,
going over it all once again,
getting ready for next time,
that magic time
when everything you bet on
comes in,
just to put life straight,
just to show who's in control,
going over the consensus,
speed, pace, consistency,
money earned,
it's all there,
just around the corner,
the eternal secret.
better hurry,
the time is short,
you've seen 70,000 races,
many of the jocks you knew
are now dead,
better hurry, Chinaski,
don't drop the whip,
go for the opening,
the wire is rushing up
at you
sitting in your room
in your undershirt
on a hot summer night,
cigarette dangling,
it has to be madness,
it was always

madness,
this endless search for the
ultimate
truth that
still can't be
stopped.

the big one

he buys 5 cars a month, details them, waxes and buffs
them out, then
resells them at a profit of one or two grand.

he has a nice Jewish wife and he tells me that he
bangs her until the walls shake.

he wears a red cap, squints in the light, has a regular
job besides the car gig.

I have no idea of what he is trying to accomplish and maybe he
doesn't either.

he's a nicer fellow than most, always good to see him,
we laugh, say a few bright lines.

but
each time
after I see him
I get the blues for him, for me, for all of us:

for want of something to do

we keep slaying our small dragons

as the big one waits.

the parade

the waving of hands, the posturing of the
limbs in putrid whiteness,
the mouth without words, the eyes without
light—
such a farce, never a farce such as this!
boulevards of human waste on parade!
look at them!
look!
god, I'm going to puke out my battered damned
heart at the sight of them!
these awful disgusting creatures posing as
this or that—
a king, a bathing beauty, a dancer,
a clown, a mouse …
Christ, stop it!
the walls are falling!
this darkness shakes me like a dirty rag!
human waste on parade throughout the
centuries!
why am I the last one alive?
there's no answer to
that.

bum on the loose

I climbed off a park bench to engage the giants of
literature in battle.
I lived with women madder than the gods
themselves.
I consumed enough booze to get an army drunk.
I lived in shacks without windows, without electricity,
without plumbing, without heat.
I climbed off the park bench to engage the giants of
literature in battle.
I was beaten in alleys, robbed.
I searched the cities for sanity.
I read great books and they made me sleepy.
I starved in rooms fat with rats.
my parents were in shame of me.
the beautiful ladies thought me ugly.
I climbed off the park bench to engage the giants of
literature in battle.
the world considered me insane.
I slept in deserted graveyards.
I sat in bars through the mornings and into the night
and back into morning.
I engaged the giants of literature.
all my work came back.
one editor wrote, "what is this stuff?"
I worked the factories, the warehouses.
I got married and divorced.
I was 40 years old when my first thin pamphlet of poems was
published.
it wasn't that good.
at the age of 50 I decided to become a professional writer.
I earned $980 the first year.
I lived on a candy bar a day.
I was engaging the giants of literature.
the ladies descended like locusts.
I threw people off my front porch.
I was engaging the giants.
the giants were not aware of this.
only I was aware.

I climbed off the park bench to engage the giants of literature.

I didn't think that they were all that good.

tell me, do you?

going away

down through the last door,
past the music,
past the dancing girls,
down through the last hall
past the last New Year
and the last hurrah!
past the flight of the
hummingbird,
past the last kiss,
the last flux and flow,
the last new day,
the last night's sleep,
the last sweet orange,
the last war,
past the last
last
word.

stag

this guy pretended to be a French painter
and I sat on a couch with a beer
then 2 girls walked in
while he
the painter
was asleep in a chair
drunk

one of the girls
took his cock out and stroked it

while the other one
painted it
(on canvas, that is)

and then he awakened and the girls began to
strip down

and the painter had the 2 girls and this one
cock, and he did it all
while they did it
all

and sometimes it was difficult to
separate the 3 bodies
and I sat there while the camera focused
and I thought, hell, we're all
crazy,

and when it was all over
everybody got dressed and I was
introduced to the
actors. (actresses too, pardon me,
girls.)

the guy with the cock was trying to log enough hours
to be a commercial airline
pilot.

162

one of the girls—the *young* looking one—
had a girl in college

the other one wanted to go to the Orient and
study something or
other.

the cameraman
poured the whiskey around
and we sat there laughing and enjoying
each other.

they made their living with stag films
and it was a little studio room
#228
someplace in Hollywood

but I got the feeling that if I pulled out my cock
everybody would be
insulted, even
I

so I had a few more drinks
got a phone
from one of the girls for
later

and drove on
home.

late payment

a rifle bullet across the page and into Shakespeare's
grave,
the steam iron pressed against the inner
arm,
the headless scream,
the unfolding dahlia,
notes from a dirty diary,
the lion's nightmare at 2:30 p.m.,
this summer has run through the trees like a tank,
I jam my heart into a rubber glove and the fingers JUMP,
the Russian Empire gurgles down the garbage drain,
we approach the 21st Century with our dirty stinking laundry,
the gods are done with me and them and this,
the last useless word looking for a place to die.

2 horse collars

I'm hot now, he said,
and lined a single to
center.
next up he tripled,
then drew a walk,
4th at bat
he homered.
5th at bat
he doubled.

I'm hot now, he said,
then sang in the
shower.
when he got to his
place
his woman wasn't
there.

he went to the dresser drawer
got what he needed
went over to Mike's and
broke the door down.
they were in bed
together.
at the last moment
he got the real truth of it,
changed his mind
put the gun into his mouth
and pulled the
trigger.

the next day they had the rookie
up from Memphis in his
spot. the kid went 0 for 4,
suckered on the change-up
and the low and inside fast ball.
but he was good with the women
and that's more important than
.364

counsel

I am living in hell, he told me, and I said, is that right,
Frankie? and he said, I am truly living in hell, you
would never believe it.
everything, he continued, has hardened into a repetitious
march to nowhere.
is that right, Frankie? fucking-a, he said, you ever
been locked into a situation where the only escape is
death?
yes, I told him.
then what do you do? he asked.
Frankie, I just wait, death is coming anyhow.
but, he told me, I can't wait.
Frankie, you'll wait.
why, asked me, is pain the most present and constant
thing in life?
physical pain is hard to explain, Frankie, but I know what
causes most spiritual pain.
yeah? yeah? he asked.
most spiritual pain, my lad, is caused by
too much expectation.
yeah? yeah? he asked.
too much expectation, I said, try to avoid it.
do you? he asked.
yes, more and more I expect less and less.
and do you get less?
almost always, Frankie.
damn, he said, it always helps to talk to you, you've been
around the block.
I'm afraid so, Frankie.
he asked, did you ever think you would live this long?
Frankie, I haven't lived this long, I've lasted this
long, good
night.

I hung up the receiver and pulled the
bottle
toward me.

166

the fighter

Hemingway feels it in the grave
every time the bulls run through
the streets of
Pamplona
again

he sits up
the skeleton rattles

the skull wants a drink

the eyeholes want sunlight, action.

the young bulls are beautiful,
Ernest

and you were
too

no matter
what they say

now.

my worst rejection slip

came to me when I was living in
that court on DeLongpre.
it was from the editor of one
of the sex mags on
Melrose Avenue.

"listen, Bukowski, you are a
good writer but *never*
send us a story like that
again!
no man beds down with
that many women
in a day or in a night
and a day,
especially an ugly old
fart like you!
we've been delighted
with your previous
fiction
but
please, please,
please,
don't lay the bullshit
on too thick,
the reader will
never believe
it
and we here
are insulted to
the *god-damned*
hilt with your
exaggerations!"

well, I reread the
story and found it
perfectly accurate
in the factual
sense.

I dropped it on the
floor and went in
and poured a
drink.
as I walked out
there was a
knock on the
door.

it was a young lady.
she stood there
looking
wild.

"what are you
doing?"

"nothing."

"well, I'm taking
Nina to visit her father
and then I'm
coming right
back!"

"oh good, baby ..."

then she turned
and ran to
her
car,
I heard it roar
off down the
street.

I slammed the
drink down and
then the
phone rang.

"hello," I
said.

it was a female
voice.

"what are you
doing?"

"nothing."

"are you drinking?"

"yes."

"is there a woman
there with you?"

"no."

"we were to have
dinner together
and you were
going to spend the
night.
do you
remember?"

"sure, baby,
I'll be there at
seven."

she hung
up.

I sat down with
my drink.
I finished it.
then I got up
and got another,

sat there.

there was a knock
on my door.
it was my landlady.
she was already
red-faced with
booze.

"o.k.," she said,
"I've got twelve
quarts of
Eastside in
the refrigerator.
you comin'
down?"

"later …"

"you better come
down, you horny old son-of-
a-bitch!"

"oh, I will …"

then she was
gone.
and I looked down
at the rejected
story
on the floor.

too bad,
the way people
thought:
that only handsome
young men
got all the
action.
and I didn't even

want the
action.
it was getting between
me
and my
typewriter.

it's true that there
were days
when nobody
bothered me.
then I sometimes
masturbated.

those were the days
when I got my
work done.

I picked the story up
and slipped it back
into the
envelope for the
time
being.

later on
I'd mail it off to
somebody with
more common
sense.

40,000

now
at the track today,
Saturday,
Father's Day,
each paid admission is
entitled to a free wallet
and each wallet contains a
little surprise.

most of the men are
between 30 and 55,
going to fat,
many of them in walking
shorts.
they have gone stale in mid-
life,
flattened out.

men like
these don't even
deserve death,
these little walking
whales,
only there are so
many of
them,
in the urinal,
in the food lines,
the species has managed to
survive
in a most limited
sense
and when you see
so many of them
like that,
up close,
there but not there,
breathing, farting,

commenting,
waiting for the thunder
that will not be heard,
waiting for the charging
white horse of
Glory,
waiting for the lovely
female who will not
arrive,
waiting to WIN,
waiting for the great
dream to
engulf them
you can only wonder.

they clomp in their
sandals,
gulp at hot dogs
animal style,
gulping the
meat.
they complain about
losing,
blame the jocks,
drink green
beer.
the parking lot is
jammed with their
mortgaged
cars.

the jocks mount once
again for another
race,
the men press
toward the betting
windows
mesmerized,
fathers and non-fathers,
Monday is waiting

for them,
and this is the last
big lark.

but at the same time
in that same place
the horses are
totally
beautiful.
it is shocking how
beautiful they
are
at that time,
in that place,
their life shines
through them:
miracles happen,
even in
hell.

I decide to stay for
one more
race.

coffeeshop

she has served me and I am
eating,
"is everything all right?"
she asks.
"yes, thank you…"
"more coffee?"
"all right …"

I am reading the paper
and eating.
"cream?" she asks.
"no, thanks…"

she pours the
coffee.

5 minutes pass.
she is back
"is everything all right?"
"yes."
"more coffee?"
"no."
"are you going to try
one of our desserts?"
"no, thank you…"
"come on, you only
live once!"
"yes, I know …"

she leaves again.
but not for long.

"you care for more
rolls?"
"no, thank you…"
"did you like the
turkey?"
"yes."

"you ought to try
our roast beef."
"you mean,
now?"
"no, next time."

she just stands there.
"I saw you in here the
other day with your
daughter."
"that was my wife."
"oh, you're married…"
"yes."
"more coffee?"
"all right."
"you take cream?"
"no cream."

she comes back and
pours the
coffee.
then leaves.

I try it.
it's unbearably
strong.
they don't clean the
coffee maker.

it's time to leave,
I need the bill.
I look for the waitress.
I don't see her
anywhere.
I read the paper:
mass murderer boils
the heads for
soup.

the bus boy comes

by,
picks up my
plate,
leaves the bad
coffee.

then he comes back
carrying the coffee
container.

"more coffee?"

"no, thanks, have you seen
the waitress?"

"no."

"where is she?"

"I don't know."

he walks off.

I sit waiting.
nobody appears.

I get up from the
table to go look for
the waitress.
I find her just outside
the kitchen,
she's smoking a
cigarette and talking
to the cook.

"waitress," I ask,
"can I have the
check?"

"oh yes," she

smiles.

I go back and sit
down.
she arrives with the
check.
she's signed her
name at the
bottom,
"thanks!
Carolyn."
she has drawn a
little smiling
face.
she puts the check down
on top of a wet
spot.

"more coffee?"

"no, thanks."

"was everything all
right?"

"yes."

she walks off.
I leave a tip, go to
the register,
pay the bill.
the owner is
behind the
register.
she takes my
money, hands me
the change
without looking at
me.
she is an older

woman,
a bit on the
heavy
side.
still looking at
something else in front
of her
she asks,
"was everything
all right?"
"yes," I answer
and I go out the
door and into the
street and into the
world,
never to return
there again,
not in this life
or any life.
I find my car,
get in, drive away
thinking, now if
that wasn't hell
then hell isn't going to
be
so bad.

poetry readings

poetry readings have to be some of the saddest
damned things ever,
the gathering of the clansmen and clanladies,
week after week, month after month, year
after year,
getting old together,
reading on to tiny gatherings,
still hoping their genius will be
discovered,
making tapes together, discs together,
sweating for applause
they read basically to and for
each other,
they can't find a New York publisher
or one
within miles,
but they read on and on
in the poetry holes of America,
never daunted,
never considering the possibility that
their talent might be
thin, almost invisible,
they read on and on
before their mothers, their sisters, their husbands,
their wives, their friends, the other poets
and the handful of idiots who have wandered
in
from nowhere.

I am ashamed for them,
I am ashamed that they have to bolster each other,
I am ashamed for their lisping egos,
their lack of guts.

if these are our creators,
please, please give me something else:

a drunken plumber at a bowling alley,

a prelim boy in a four rounder,
a jock guiding his horse through along the
rail,
a bartender on last call,
a waitress pouring me a coffee,
a drunk sleeping in a deserted doorway,
a dog munching a dry bone,
an elephant's fart in a circus tent,
a 6 p.m. freeway crush,
the mailman telling a dirty joke

anything
anything
but
these.

4

twisting the cap off the tube
of night

journey to the end

there is this fellow in the Netherlands who sends
me photos of Celine and boxes of marvelous
cigars.
well, I am a dog: I enjoy both.
the cigars go well with my red wine and I never tire of
Celine or his photos—a very good face on that fellow
Louis Ferdinand Destouches.
(we have some famous modern writers whose faces look like
the inside of bedpans and they write the same way.)

I like my nights with Celine's photos,
classical music, cigars, red wine and the
computer.

Celine watches over me as I drink, type, listen to music
and smoke the cigars; we have a great time together as
other people are bowling, sleeping, watching tv, arguing,
screwing, eating, doing all those
dumb things and others.

and now here
the words fly like crazy sparrows in a storm, Shostakovich
bellows from the radio, as the cigar smoke whirls to the left and
out
the door and into a night as dark as red wine.

hello Celine…Celine…you dog…we endure the pain
of centuries…but we can laugh…sometimes. here
among your photos the
dark luck is good.

upon reading a critical review

it's difficult to accept
and you look around the room
for the person they are talking
about.

he's not there.
he's not here.
he's gone.

by the time they get to your books you
are no longer in your
books.
you are on the next page,
in your next
book.

and worse,
they don't even get the old books right.
you are given credit you don't
deserve, for insights that aren't
there.

people read *themselves* into books, altering
what they need and discarding what they
don't.

good critics are as rare as good
writers.
and whether I get a good review or a
bad one
I can take neither
seriously.

I am on the next page.
in the next book.

the beautiful lady

we are gathered here now
to bury her in this
poem.

she did not marry an unemployed wino who
beat her every
night.

her several children will never wear
snot-stained shirts
or torn dresses.

the beautiful lady
simply
calmly
died.

and may the clean dirt of this poem
bury
her.

her and her womb
and her jewels
and her combs and her
poems

and her pale blue eyes
and her
grinning
rich
frightened
husband.

black

there are nights so bad
that the fingers on the
keys are
useless
and you might as well
cover the
machine,
might as well
sit in a chair,
go to
bed,
wait on life,
wait on death,
wait on change.

literature is
just no damned
good
now,
yours or
anybody
else's.

my style

I watch the jocks come out in the post parade
and one will win the race, the others will lose
but each jock must win sometime in some race
on some day, and he must do it often enough
or he is no longer a jockey.

it's like each of us sitting over a typewriter
tonight or tomorrow or next week or next month.
it's like the girls on the street trying to score
for their pimps
and they have to do it often enough
or they are no longer whores
and we have to do it often enough
or we're whores who can't score.

I would like a little more kindness and warmth
in the structure of things.

I became a writer but when I was a boy
I used to dream of becoming the village idiot,
I used to lie in bed and imagine myself that careless idiot,
planning ways to get food and sympathy easily,
a planned confusion of not too much love or
effort.

some would claim that I have succeeded
in this.

dead

he wrote a joyous and mad
novel about unbelievable and
romantic episodes
and his words danced with
laughter and mockery and
gamble.

the novel made him
famous and he went on
to write others but none
like the first.

then he stopped
writing, came here from
his native land
and became a professor
at a southern
university.

he wears his suit, his
tie, his dignity
as tokens of
respectability
as his students wait
for him to go wild,
to break down the
walls,
to smash glass,
precedence,
minds.

but the semesters
pass, quiet
seasons.

R.I.P.

a re-evaluation

he told me he
had 6 kids
had been
married
5 times and that next
Wednesday
he would be
38 years
old.

I had always thought of him
as
one of the sharpest
valets at
racetrack
parking

but then
I've always been better at
picking horses
than at
picking
people.

snake-eyes

William Saroyan
married the same
woman
twice

which means
he must have
forgotten
something
about the
first
time
around.

anyhow, he claimed
it ruined his
life.

but,
actually,
there are
many things
which can
ruin
a man's
life

just
depending upon
which one
gets to him
first.

our world

it's strange, isn't it?
you can't
compare it to
anything
else
yet you quickly
learn
that there is
something wrong
with it
and with the people
that
inhabit it.

you want to
be objective
and fair
but when you
see what it
does to us
and the choices
it leaves
us—
the streets you must
walk,
what you hear
and see,
endure
day by day
year by year,
night and
day—
god damn it,
you have nothing to
compare *that* with
either
so you really
can't call it
awful

but why does
it seem
to be?

for example
putting
your shoes on
in the morning
is like having
to walk
through
mountains.

yes,
it must be
us.
we must be
sick.
that must
be
it
although we have
nothing to
compare us
with
either.

sick.
unperceptive.
born into this wondrous
light and
glory
and then gagging
on it,
puking it
away
as the bees
and the butterflies
transport
ever more,
their bloody
pollen.

how to get rid of the purists

several months ago I was sent some tapes
by a musician who had put several of
my poems to music.
he professed much interest in my
poesy.
I played the tapes on the way to the track
and back.
very classical (and I am a classical music
freak)
but the overall tone of the work was
I felt
tinged with intellectual
elitism—the pretentious soprano voices and the
general presentation.

I was both abashed and honored that
the composer had lent so much effort and
musical learning to my work.
at the same time I felt that the overall
effect was anti-life, anti-me, anti-the-
clarity of directly seeking joy, pain,
anything reasonable or
sufficient.
it was the same old con, the same old
snobbism, the same old murderous kiss
of death clothed in a creative
act.

so I wrote the gentleman back, "you know,
I have certain problems, one of them
being with instruments.
some instruments which I dislike
are the piano, the violin and the soprano
voice, especially the latter.
the human voice besides being basically
ugly also reminds me of the human
race
and one of the last things I want to

think of and one of the first things I
want to get away from when I listen to
classical music is
the human
race.
I write for the same reason.
is it possible that you can rewrite this
whole thing
without using the above-mentioned
instruments?"

I haven't heard from this composer
since.
which is part of my plan.
the other part being to antagonize,
deplete, expose and shame
the thousands of practitioners of
the arts in all of their forms
who have been subsidized by
snobbery, dullness, and the willful
push toward fame
which has left us with
centuries of accepted
and immensely admired
works of
art of
which
all too many
are surely
useless,
worthless,
fake
and so supremely boring
that we think that
they certainly must be
something
real.

a curious thing

I have known a great many women
and one common little quirk
that I have
noticed
occurs most often when eating
out.
I will be speaking
and perhaps it will not be
vitally interesting
but the lady will suddenly
turn her face away from me,
and will gaze across the
room intently
at a group at another
table.
most often I will simply
stop what I am
saying and wait for
her attention to
return.
at other times I will say,
"oh, is it somebody you
know?"
or,
"is it something
interesting?"
"no," they will
answer.
and if the lady then
rises and goes to
the restroom
I will check the group
at the table
who stole her
attention
and see only a bevy
of quite common
dolts.

or
I will be speaking
and a group will
enter and as
they walk by
her attention will shift
and her eyes will
feast on them
as if she had seen
something
extraordinary.
I don't bother to
check out these
newcomers myself.
I feel their
death-glow
as they walk
past.

now, what I
mean to say here is that
I might often be
a bore
and not worth
listening to
but then I wonder
why the ladies
are there with
me in the
first
place?

I will admit
that often as they
converse with me
I find their
conversation
vapid or
worse
but I hear them

out,
often interjecting a
little nod
or an affirmation
such as, "yes…"
or a simple
"uh huh…"
but I never turn
directly away
and focus my attention
elsewhere
especially in
mid-speech.

when they take their
attention away
like that
I do believe that
they think that they
are being
worldly and
observant.
but it's terribly
clear.
don't they know
I can
read this
behavior?

it's true that people
can be together
too much,
too long,
it can be awful,
it can be a bore
and a
grind.
and then when I suggest
to the lady
that perhaps we had

best forget the
whole matter and
go our separate
ways,
once again
I get a common
reaction:
"WHAT DO YOU MEAN?"
then there are
tears.
as if all
that has occurred
had not
occurred,
as if all was sweet
and
well.

but the continual
nuances cannot
be ignored.
all disinterest isn't
sexual.

"YOU ARE A BASTARD!
YOU ARE A HORRIBLE
MAN!"

yes, yes, yes I am
and the gods and the
ladies have made
me so.

the finger

the drivers of automobiles
have very little recourse or
originality.
when upset with
another
driver
they often give him the
FINGER.

I have seen two adult
men,
florid of face
driving along
giving each other the
FINGER.

well, we all know what
this means, it's no
secret.

still, this gesture is
so overused it has
lost most of its
impact.

some of the men who give
the FINGER are captains of
industry, city councilmen,
insurance adjusters,
accountants and/or the just plain
unemployed.
no matter.
it is their favorite
response.

people will never admit
that they drive
badly.

the FINGER is their
reply.

I see grown men
FINGERING each other
throughout the day.

it gives me pause.
when I consider
the state of our cities,
the state of our states,
the state of our country,
I begin to
understand.

the FINGER is a mind-
set.
we are the FINGERERS.
we give it
to each other.
we give it coming and
going.
we don't know how
else to respond.

what a hell of a way
to not
live.

don't forget

there is always somebody or something
waiting for you,
something stronger, more intelligent,
more evil, more kind, more durable,
something bigger, something better,
something worse, something with
eyes like the tiger, jaws like the shark,
something crazier than crazy,
saner than sane,
there is always something or somebody
waiting for you
as you put on your shoes
or as you sleep
or as you empty a garbage can
or pet your cat
or brush your teeth
or celebrate a holiday
there is always somebody or something
waiting for you.

keep this fully in mind
so that when it happens
you will be as ready as possible.

meanwhile, a good day to
you
if you are still there.
I think that I am—
I just burnt my fingers on
this
cigarette.

last call

totally written out at 2 a.m.
but not worried about picking up a
lady
or driving home in a police
car.
all I have to do is to toddle into
the next room
flop on the bed
and sleep it away.
the good wife will check my
breathing.
you can end safe
but you can't start safe.
you've got to earn your stripes
first
with the gods.
and even then
you can't stay safe too
long.
I'll go crazy at least
4 more times before I
earn my gravestone,
but meanwhile
I'll toddle off
as the gods smile
and say,
"Jesus Christ, is this the same
guy who fought monsters
in dark alleys for the mere sake
of
entertainment?"

there's some damn fool
out there
who will take my
place
one
day.

meanwhile, look, there's a
gulp of beer left
and an upside-down
universe.

you be safe for a while,
I'll cut the swath.

you can't all be me
but at least
try not to be
them.
please.

undecent

brisk, brisk, brisk.
bullets and lives.
shot.

as the blackbird
sits on the
wire.

as department
store neckties
wait to be sold.

as you think of
something
as nothing
thinks of you.

the kite floats
in the wind
and the mad-
man
is right.

one of those

Sartre was some fellow, oh yes,
he showed us the bone of
Nowhere and shook it in
our face.
the choice
is yours,
he said,
morals died with God,
you're on your
own.

every now and then,
during the passing centuries,
some giant among men
arises,
shakes us truly,
shocks us out of our
sleep,
so that, at least for a
time, we become aware,
renewed
as we put our shoes on in
the morning,
as we trundle through our
tasks,
as we eat, defecate,
imagine love,
mail letters,
drive and walk the
city,
things and thoughts
assume different
shapes.

Sartre was one of those
giants.
Paris, France, much of the
world

rumbled and bounced
because of
him.

without some like him,
putting your shoes on in
the morning
would become so difficult
as to be almost
impossible.

Jean Paul,
thanks
for
everything.

candy-ass

the best part is that
after you have written 6 or 7 good poems in
one night
you can celebrate,
play,
write a candy-ass poem.
you can deliberately try to be bad,
that's fun,
most do it without trying.

that anger you?
good.
hope it makes your mother angry
too.
many mothers get angry about what I
write.
when they stop getting angry I'm
going to pack it in,
join the boy scouts.
my mother-in-law says to my
wife,
"but WHY does he have to use the
LANGUAGE he does?"
well, dear, it's just to piss you
off, get your anger up.

life has abused me and I have mis-
used it.
I enjoy attacking the sun with a
squirt gun.
I am drunk, I will sleep on my left
side to awaken in the morning and
read this candy-ass poem,
wretchedly.

the word

the word has no legs or eyes,
has no mouth, has no arms,
has no intestines and
often no heart, or very
little.

you can't ask the word to
light your cigarette
although it will help you
enjoy your wine.

and you can't force the word
to do anything it doesn't
want to do.
you can't overwork it.
and you can't awaken it
when it decides to
sleep.

the word will treat you well
at times,
depending upon what you
ask it to
do.
other times, it will treat
you badly
no matter what you ask
it to
do.

the word comes and
goes.
sometimes you must
wait a very long time
for it.
sometimes it never
comes back.

sometimes writers
kill themselves
when the word
leaves.
other writers will
pretend that it is still
there
even though the word
is dead and
buried.

many famous writers
do this.
and many less-famous
who
only call themselves
writers.

the word is not for
everybody.
and for most,
it's there
just for a very short
time.

the word is one of
the most
powerful miracles
in
existence,
it can enlighten or
destroy
minds,
nations,
cultures.

the word is dangerous
and beautiful.

if it arrives for you,

you will know
it
and you will be the
luckiest of
humans.
nothing else will
matter and
everything else will
matter.

you will be the
center of the
sun,
you will be laughing
through the
centuries,
you will have
it,
your fingers
your guts
will have
it,
you will be,
for as long as it
lasts,
a god-damned
writer
doing the possible
impossible,
getting it down,
getting it down,
getting it
down.

please

save me from them
and their smooth comfortable faces
and their relaxed
effrontery,
their crossed legs and their canvas
shoes,
their soft bellies, their soft
minds,
their cagey courtesy,
their pallid smiles,
their needless tinkering with your
hours,
their entrance into your life
through others,
god, the awful people you must
deal with
because you no longer live
alone,
these pieces of squash,
these polliwogs,
these suckerfish
and their unendurable
visitations,
there by the blinds,
nibbling bits of food,
savoring the wine,
sitting their dumb asses upon
the commodes,
staying an extra day,
an extra week,
an extra life,
so content,
wallowing in your
sight,
saved from your fury through
circumstance,
they fatten before you
stuffing their mouths with

213

olives, fruit and chips,
smiling through wine-wet lips …

others must see something in
them,
need something from
them
while I shudder in
my damned guts
in disbelief
at what confronts
me.

they notice nothing,
yawn,
and stretch their legs
through my
space.

good night, sweet prince

music of the worm
handles me like a hot fly
as escalators turn into spoons

grandma moses would have wanted it
thus—
early to rise with
tear-stained eyes

let me take you away from all this:
there is a place behind the hills
where trees are shaped like
guillotines
and mandolins have mouths like
broken bottles

a franc is worth one hundred centimes in
Luxembourg
my daughter will die in
2037
I will die in 1998
and flying fish will still continue to
fly.

Dreiser wasn't so hot either

he is really a nice fellow
of good heart
but I don't know what to do
with him:
he is bitten by too much
enthusiasm.

and I have no desire to
hurt him.

he phones often.

"I'm working on my novel," he'll
say.

"good," I'll
answer.

"123 pages..."

"good..."

"you remember what you told
me?" he will
say.

"what?"

" 'never write until you really
have to, never write until it
leaps on you and grabs you
by the throat.' "

"yes..."

"I waited and now I'm up to
page
123..."

then he'll talk about other
things, and then
a lot more about the
novel.
then it will be
over.

"was that Harry?" my wife will
ask.

"yes, it was Harry..."

a day or so will pass,
I'll drive in from
the track
and my wife will
say, "Harry phoned."

"ah..."

"he talked about his
novel..."

"123 pages..."

"135 pages...he also
said he created
a couple of
new
characters."

"yes, he told me and
I told him that it was
all right: it's
fiction..."

"he tells us both the
same things," my wife
says.

"yes..."

usually Harry phones
in the mornings, I only
wish he'd wait until
nightfall
but
he's excited.

it could be a good
novel, maybe it
is, I hope so,
only
I wish he wouldn't
talk about it
all the
time.

"I wish he wouldn't talk
about
the novel," I tell my
wife.

"why don't you tell
him?"

"Christ, I can't totally
discourage this
guy!"

"he likes you,
so tell him ..."

"look, F. Scott Fitzgerald used
to read his stuff
to his woman
right after he wrote
it.
that's
even worse than

talking about
it."

"but
you once said
F. Scott Fitzgerald
was the most over-rated
writer of
our time..."

"I just can't tell Harry
to
stop talking about
his novel," I reply.

"he's your friend..."

"maybe he's *your* friend,"
I tell her.

"but
I'm no writer..."

"for this," I tell her,
"let us bless the
gods and everything
else."

cruising

totally mentally ripped,
driving the streets in the afternoon,
stopping at signals,
looking at people walking on the
sidewalks,
it's reality but a reality that has
faded away.
you know your judgment is
warped but you don't give a
damn.
too long on earth, that's it,
that's your problem.
a story told too often.

the signal changes and you
cross the avenue,
enter a side street,
drive along
the houses are small and
sad,
have no heart.
the asphalt boils under
your wheels
and there's no place to
go,
no surprise, no wonder-
ment.

too long on earth, old
dog, you are dirtied with
life.

you circle back to the
avenue,
park behind a taco
stand, get out,
walk to the counter,
wait.

a heavy girl approaches.
she stands, looks at
you.
you pretend to be
composed.
"coffee," you say,
"small, black …"

she smiles at you.
the smile says:
I know you're crazy
but it's all
right.

you get the coffee,
take it back to the
car.
you are facing a
dirty dark yellow
wall.
you sip the
coffee:
bitter horrible
swill.

you drink half a
cup, dump it out the
window, back out of
there
and then you're
driving west.

a psychiatrist won't
help,
a psychologist won't
help,
a god won't
help.
drinking's old
and drugs make it

worse.

you just drive in your
car.
for a hundred years.
for centuries.
your head ripped
rising up through
the sun
roof
lolling on a long snake
neck
smiling a bloody
smile,
paradise at
last.

the way it is

almost everybody here is on
drugs
but the real pros
continue to function
all day and into the
night,
handling their affairs,
getting their clean laundry,
paying some of the
bills,
going on,
like that,
it's a comedy,
almost an accepted
way of life.
this neighborhood is
full of them,
they walk in and out of their
houses and jump into their
cars, they appear to be
ordinary citizens
unless you really
know them.
they have children,
they vote sometimes,
they watch tv,
they appear to be
normal citizens
and what they are
finally becomes normal
for them,
hundreds of people
in this neighborhood
drugged
continually.
it's a quietly accepted
fact.
they need the stuff to

go on,
we all know this
but nothing is ever
said about it
as the police
(paid by
the taxes of the
users)
bust the
asses of the
sellers
in this quiet
lovely
little
neighborhood.

a final word on no final word

near the end of the interview he leaned forward and
asked, "now is there any final word you'd like to leave with
your audience?"

"no," I answered, "no final word."

I felt his disappointment.

"no final word?" he asked again.

"no," I said.

he had wanted a nice closer, he had wanted me to save
his ass,
he had wanted me to save the ass of my audience.
well, I had worked hard enough to save my own ass.

"o.k.," he recovered himself and said to me, "it's been
a real pleasure to interview
you."

"sure, baby," I said.

then he motioned to the camera and sound men that
it was over
and they began packing their
gear.

"you fellows care for a drink?" I asked.

"no thanks." the interviewer spoke for everybody, they were
pulling plugs from the walls, folding equipment into
cases, it was as if I no longer
existed.

they had what they needed.

I stood with cigar and drink and watched them file out

the door and into the night.

then they were gone with their asses that needed saving
even worse than mine.

each man's hell is different

I get reports about a dear friend in
Europe, this man is not the complaining
type
so what I've learned doesn't come from
him
but he can't hide everything
and some of it filters through from other
sources:
he must go to the hospital every other
day, he is dying by the god-damned
inch.
his home life has long been
unhappy
and now
his wife has become
suicidal.
most of my letters to him
go unanswered
and when he does
reply
the responses are clipped and
stark.

I've learned he can't drink, smoke,
ever consume coffee
and
there are
occupational
problems.

he's not old.

my friend always wanted to be
a writer
he became a translator
working the language of the
successful practitioners
into his own.

the long hard hours
with the dream
getting further
and further out of
reach,
his wife going
mad:

"you're always
typing!"

a killing unhappiness:
never knowing
what you might have
been.

the powers that be

there was a crowd at this dinner.
they were all telling jokes of
one sort or another,
some of them were professional
actors, directors of note, writers,
and it gave me a little
tingle to be with such talented
humans.
there was a lull, finally,
and I began telling about something
that was not a joke.
about something that had happened to me.
I mean, I wasn't serious but at the
same time I was serious,
trying to explain what
had occurred, about
something that might occur
unexpectedly in any man's life,
something to be understood,
something to cherish.
I guess it was
a rather philosophical story
informed by decades of
my living life out.

then, I was finished.
there was silence.
nobody agreed or disagreed.
and then, at once, they all began
again
chatting about
little happenings,
the waiter appeared and
disappeared,
desserts and libations,
further in-jokes and out-jokes,
the candles flickered in their
glass enclosures,

eyes locked and unlocked,
lips opened,
mouths smiled, hands
gestured,
these were the talented minds that
informed our way,
these were the talented minds that
informed their way.
I was sitting with talented
shit.

clever

the clever people slide downstream like
white fish
through the blue water,
past the rapids,
the clever people
with their clever throats and eyebrows,
their clever nostril hairs,
both shoes laced,
all dooms erased,
teeth white,
the clever people slide cleanly,
even their deaths are one-tenth deaths,
clever clever clever,
they have better walls,
better cars,
a better way to laugh.
even their nightmares are ringed with
tinsel,
these clever ones,
they sit across from you,
whitely smiling,
full of it,
even the hair on their head
glints cleanly.
how long have I lived and looked
upon them.
do you know what death really is?
it's one of these clever
cocksuckers
shaking your hand and
embracing
you.
you know what death really
is?
come see me
as I slip the Gold Card
to the waiter
while

disliking
you. or
worse.

the poem

they all keep publishing poems
but it's doubtful what a
poem can really accomplish.

centuries of poems
and we're back to the
starting point.

like philosophy, history,
medicine, science, poems seem to
alter things,
seem to lead toward a way
out
then falter against the
changing currents and increasing
odds.

a poem is no better than a
good can opener,
a spare tire,
or
aspirin for a
headache.

the poem isn't much
but let me tell you
if I hadn't discovered
it
I would be dead
or
you would be dead
or many people
would be
dead
or
if not dead
then horribly
mutilated

in one sense or
another.

still, a poem can only
be a poem.

lines like these

floating on a page

burning holes in the face of
death

twisting the cap off the tube
of
night

following the dog of summer
to the end of his
rope.

huh?

my mail

keeps evolving and there is more
of it.
in the old days
many letters were from ladies,
often with photos.
I'd tell them to come visit
and I met them at the airport
and drove them
home.
then there was drinking and
sex.
most stayed two or three days,
then left.

there were also letters from
men in jail, some as far away as
Australia.
I answered these letters.
there were also letters from
poets, known and
unknown.
then there were a few mental
cases.
I answered these as well.
the problem was that they all
wanted continual
response,
a life-long correspondence.
when I would inform them
that this couldn't be done
I received some irrational
and foul responses
in return.

I found myself writing dozens
of letters a
month.
and my intention

as a writer had not been to
correspond with
any and
all.

I finally gave up
babying my
mailbox.

I read my mail but in
90 percent of the cases
I didn't
respond.

I heard a story about
Faulkner.
when he got a letter
he held it up to the
light.
if he didn't see a check
in there
he threw it away
unopened.

I read my mail
then threw it
away.

now much of my mail
is from college
professors.
some of them are
precise and pleasant
enough
but few are worthy
of response.

and there are a couple of
self-published books of poetry
a week,

few worthy of
response.

the ladies and the
convicts and the madmen
have dropped
away.

I still get letters from
people who announce they will
soon be in town to
"drink 8 or ten beers" with
me ...

my job
as a writer
is to write.
I am not a counselor
nor an entertainer,
nor am I interested in
reading books of
poesy
or bedding down
or giving blurbs
or recommending unsung
so-called geniuses
to my
publisher.

when I was an unknown
writer
I sent my work
directly to the magazines
and the publishers,
never with a cover
letter,
and I never knocked on
anybody's
door
and I never read my

work to my wives or
my girlfriends
or anybody.

when you are in a prize fight
you climb into the
ring,
you do it where it is
done.
and it's not done at
literary parties or by
writing Burroughs or
Mailer
or Ferlinghetti.

you sit down at your
machine
and fire it into the
unknown,
and if you don't have
a machine
you write it on the
walls or on the edges
of newspapers.
and you'll keep doing
it,
doing it,
and if you've got
it,
the guts and the
laughter and the manner
of saying it
you'll finally come
through.
forget everything
else.

the gods are good,
they only want to
make sure.

walking with the dead

and talking with the dead and driving the freeways
with the dead and standing in the supermarket
with the dead

what the doctor ordered is
not what I ordered
not what you ordered
not what we ordered.

take the whole thing back.

throw it out.

start over again.

up through the night

the way I can tell it is the Christmas
season is that the classical
music on the radio gets
bad.
I mean with an exception or two
we are left in a musical vacuum.
music
like any other creative endeavor
must have its own personal
meaning,
must find its own way.
it can't be programmed by general
agreement
or somebody's mother-in-law's
concept of
what is appropriate
for the season.

things with their own power
and with a life of their own
go their own way
make their own statements
bring light by their own
magic.
it's what makes death
bearable and life worth
discarding.

the fool dines out

I am with others, including my wife, it is a dark and
expensive place, we order wine, high-
priced stuff, the waiter brings it, applies corkscrew,
pulls, and the prong rips out of the cork leaving
said cork within the bottle, so he reinserts the cork-
screw, tugs, and it happens again—corkscrew in
the air, cork in the bottle.

"having a little trouble, eh?" I
ask him.

my wife digs an elbow to my ribs, the waiter goes off
for another bottle, returns, digs the corkscrew in again
—same thing: out comes the corkscrew without the cork.

"you need another opener," I
suggest.

I get another dig in the ribs, the waiter glowers at me,
he's enraged, gives it another try, same result.

"wow!" I say.

the others at the table look at me as if I had just been
convicted of child-rape and now everybody is enraged
except me as the waiter goes for a third bottle, returns,
and as he inserts the corkscrew he fixes his eyes on
me and I silently (of course) wish
him luck and this time he
makes it.

I am the wine-taster, he pours me a bit, I give it a sip,
wait a moment, nod to him that the wine is all
right.

for the remainder of our stay there the other people talk
as if I am non-existent but upon hearing the
conversation I am most happy

that I am excluded.

upon leaving I pay the bill, tip 20%, and we walk to
the parking lot, the others feeling that they have acted
properly
in our civilization of expensive restaurants. they even
say goodnight to me. as the valets rush for our ex-
pensive cars I
wonder what the waiter will do with those two bottles
with the ruined corks, I always dig the corks out. drink
the wine, cork and all.

meanwhile my wife is waiting to tell me, when we are
in the car alone, that I treated the waiter quite
horribly, didn't I know how to act in public?

and I won't
reply.

hey, hey, hey

sometimes it's bad or just ordinary,
you adjust to senseless conditions,
then a new card drops out of the deck,
it severs the tendon between the thumb
and the forefinger,
a dark electric numbness overwhelms the
spinal cord
and your mother's face appears on a
billboard
skewered as it should be,
advertising
adversity as the norm,
you pour a fresh drink,
duck down between the stink of humanity
and the ferocious boredom of
time,
come up once to blink,
go down twice to think it over,
dial 911
and get a voiceless voice
like the dead scream of a
caterpillar
as Rome sculpts the monster
and children as little
as flies
crawl the walls of your
brain.

band-aid

we are destroyed by our
conscience, I explained to
him.

no, no, that's not what I
mean, he said.
I mean, I'll wake up
feeling good, you know,
ready for action, ready
for whatever's out there and
then the *first* word she'll
say to me
will be
vicious and stupid,
really unwarranted, you know.
then, I'm depressed, the
whole day's
shot through the head.

we are destroyed by expecting
more than there is,
I said.

or, he continued, I'll be out
doing my job all day, it will be hard
enough, but I'll see it through
and I'll drive up thinking, now
for the good part. I'll park,
get out, walk in the door,
and she'll say something
totally unrelated either to her
or to me, I mean something that
is simply and violently *ugly*,
you know, and there
goes the evening and the night,
there goes any good feeling
I might have had.

you sound like a nit-
pick, I said.

you mean these things don't
happen to you? he asked.
I mean, with your
woman?

never, I told him.

no problems? she respects you?
he asked.

she adores me, I said, the way
I speak, walk, talk, my
glow, the whole bundle.

I don't believe you,
he said.

you shouldn't, I
answered.

why do women act
like that? he
asked.

it's love, I answered,
they care.

maybe it would be better
if they hated us?
he asked.

they do, I said.

I just wish they'd treat us
with the same respect they
treat strangers, he
said.

we couldn't stand that,
I said.

you mean we get what we
need? he asked.

we need what we get, I
told him.

is there anything else?
he asked.

not today, I said, we've
been talking an hour—
that's $150.

I think you've
compounded my
problems, he
said.

maybe, I told him, and
that's why you should
come again
next week.
I guess so, he
said.

I'll see you then, I told
him, good
day.

the dangling carrot

the perfect poem will never be
written.

I back out the driveway at
11 a.m.,
swing around,
wave to my wife,
drive down the hill and into
the world.

the perfect poem will never be
written,
never be written
here
anywhere
on a page,
in the street,
on the wall
in Paris
in Peru
in the men's room,
in the train station,
on a billboard,
on the head of a pin,
the perfect poem will never be
written.

for this,
let us thank the gods.

preparation

you've got to burn
straight up and down
and then maybe sidewise
for a while
and have your guts
scrambled by a
bully
and the demonic
ladies,
you've got to run
along the edge of
madness
teetering,
you've got to drink a
river of booze,
you've got to starve
like a winter
alleycat,
you've got to live
with the imbecility
of at least a dozen
cities,
then maybe
maybe
maybe
you might know
where you are
for a tiny
blinking
moment.

freeway

the seven suns dimmed into one
and the last porpoise rose to
the surface
as I shifted into high
gear
while racing the man in the
white late model
Porsche.
drums banged in my brain,
the blood flowed down to
my toes
as I pushed the
accelerator
down to the floor,
I was gaining
inching up
as Mount Shasta
exploded into a
beautiful
day.

5

the big guy doesn't have me
out of here yet

the new homeless

I've
been driving down this tree-lined street for
12 years or so
on my way to wherever, past
the rich homes, the pony trails, past
the lush smell of money and
security.
but now
in these strangest of times,
parts of the structure suddenly
topple,
taking with it some of the modestly
rich
on a long
dark ride.
others remain untouched,
but in today's newspaper I read
that some of these 850,000 dollar homes
have been built over a land-
fill.
driveways are cracking,
back yards are sinking,
houses are tilting, walls and
foundations are cracking,
there are loud explosions in the
night.
there are sink-holes in the ground
from which emanate
stinking gasses which may
be poisonous and
explosive.
the trees are dying and
nothing will grow in the
yards.
the homes are un-
salable
but still taxed at the
former level.

even the pony trails are
sagging, dangerous.
the horses stay in their
collapsing stables...

these were the people
who thought they had
beat the
system,
made the educated and
intelligent
choices.

now, they are
finished.
and the builders and the
realtors
who swindled them
are long
gone
to safer, richer
climes.

America the beautiful
suddenly turned
ugly.
time after time,
in life after life,
in way after way,
some will
always be
classically
screwed.

the mail

the mail gets heavier.
more and more letters telling me
what a great writer I
am,
plus poems, novels, novelettes,
short stories, paintings.
some just want an autograph,
a drawing, a word.
others suggest an ongoing
correspondence.

I read everything, dump every-
thing, go about my
business.

I am aware that no man is
a "great" writer.
he may have been a
great writer,
but it's a process which
begins again and over
again
and all the praise,
the cigars, the bottles of
wine sent in
honor
will not get the next
line down,
and that's all that counts,
the past is
useless,
now is in the laps of
the gods
as the centuries fall
away
in their rotten
swift
luxury.

killing life

minor and trivial complaints,
constantly aired,
might drive a saint mad,
let alone a common good
old boy (me).
and worse, those who
complain
are hardly aware they do it
unless finally told
and even finally told
they don't believe it.
and so nothing leads
anywhere
and it's just another day
wasted,
kicked in the ass,
mutilated
while the Buddha
sits in the corner
smiling.

wait, it will find us

a day at the track,
followed by a swim in the
pool,
followed by 5 minutes in the
spa,
followed by a shower,
followed by opening the mail
(not very interesting
mail)
then the good wife
recounts some portion of
her day,
the seven cats greet me
one by one
and the evening has
begun.

from original hell to this.
can I bear
it?
can you?

don't worry,
hell will return, grown
stronger,
it will find me
again
older, fatter
and I will report the
matter to you,
dear reader,
in the fashion that
you have become
accustomed
to.

the x-factor

pain in back, feel bloated, should cut my
toenails,
smoking here
past midnight,
radio turned low,
warm night,
I have my view of the
freeway,
I'm still alive
but not so sure of the
others,
I keep getting approached by
strangers at the racetrack
who want to talk,
they push their faces too
close,
I am stricken by their
eyes,
they jabber away
like monkeys in a
zoo
and finally
I break away,
ride the escalator a
while,
sometimes go out to
parking,
walk in the sun,
come back,
watch another god-
damned horse
race.

I feel tired and bloated
with it
all,
thinking back
now

on the day.
yes, I won, yes.

but I've got to think of
something
else.
maybe I'll hang around
Art Museums?
no.
awful.
maybe I'll play with
paints?
ah, no.

you know, this sitting
around waiting to
die,
it's not a very kind
hobby.

I watch the smoke
drift about the
room, turn up the
radio.

I tell you, I don't mind
death
but it pisses me off
when the animals
die.

well, here I am
sitting in my shorts,
complaining
again.

and getting paid
for it.

who could have
ever guessed?

evaluation

oh yes, I'm a good guy,
as soon as the toilet paper
runs low,
I'll take it out and replace
it
with a full fat roll.
I don't live
alone
and I am aware
that a sudden unwilling search
of that dark blank
cardboard
can jinx this tender mood
or write a curse
on the cool tile
wall.

good guys like me are needed in
this more than difficult
world.

the young

I watch them going up and down the hill on their
Suzukis, gunning them, ripping the night with
sound, the lights are bright, up and down
the hill they go, it's only Thursday
night but any night will do, there's hardly
any place to go, gang territory across Pacific
Avenue and more gangs on Gaffey Street, only
a few safe blocks to play with and they park
their bikes, stand around talking, there's not
much money, they share joints and a few pills,
school tomorrow, maybe, hell, maybe not.

I stand out front watering a patch of lawn, maybe they
see me, and if they do, it doesn't matter, I'm just
another old fart in a world of old farts, yet I
feel like walking over and saying, "come on,
let's find something to do …" but I know better, I know
that they don't know any more than I do and they
are probably more scared, I had my fling
ripping at the walls, I used to stand and beat
my hands against the bricks until they bled and
I kept punching but the world stayed there
unlikeable, monstrous, deadly.

I see them talking, then shut off the water, drag
the hose back into the yard, walk up the drive
and they are left standing in the world I passed on to them, they
are hopelessly screwed, castrated, denuded.

—the passing of the torch through the centuries,
they have it now.
Thursday night, nowhere to go.
Friday night. Saturday. Sunday. Monday.
etc.
the oldest young on earth.
Thursday night. Thursday night. Thursday
night.

"come on, let's find something to do…"

no return address

I am perishable and that's the best
part
as the snail crawls slowly under
the leaf,
as the lady in the cafe
laughs an ugly laugh,
as France burns in purple
twilight.
I am perishable
and good for that
as the horse kicks a slat out of the
barn,
as we hurry toward
paradise,
I am perishable enough.
place the empty shoes beneath the
bed
side by side.
as the dog howls
the last frog puffs and
jumps.

yes sirree!

all our neighbors think that
we are
weird.
and we think that they
are.
and we're all
on
target.

snapshot (1985)

flailing away at infinity
the tiny winged night bug
on its back
under the desk lamp
kicks and struggles with
thread legs
under the heat of the
light
as in the corner of the
room
my fat yellow cat
lifts his left leg
high
and licks his precious
parts
as in the harbor now
a boat suddenly looses
a horn sound

the cat stiffens, stops
licking

the bug becomes
motionless

then,
both at once,
they return to their
former
divertissements.

finished?

the critics now have me
drinking champagne and
driving a BMW
and also married to a
socialite from
Philadelphia's Main Line
which of course
is going to prevent me
from writing my earthy
and grubby stuff.
and they might be
right,
I could be getting to be
more like them,
and that's as close to
death as you can
get.

we'll see.
but don't bury me yet.
don't worry if I drink with
Sean Penn.
just measure the poems
as they come off the
keyboard.
listen only to them.
after this long fight
I have no intention of
quitting short.
or late.
or satisfied.

the voice of Chinaski

modern composers are writing pieces using
the voice of the whale—
working it into
music.

the whale has a feeding ground of twenty
square miles
which he patrols and uses
alone

until the time comes when he starts
calling for his
mate—
then this voice is sent trumpeting through the
water

those waters of used tires and inner
tubes, old blankets and piano wire
discarded test tubes and burnt-out Spanish
bullfighters.

get lonely get
horny.

we're all caught
the same:
goldfish
dove
dog
tiger.

sometimes even mountains
move
boil out in
flame.

you have me
and the nuns and the monks have
God.

quotable

she is an old woman
now
still quite beautiful
she has known many
famous
men.

we are sitting in a Mexican cafe
and she tells me,
"Hemingway was an amazing
man, he'd sit and
make these off-hand remarks,
one after another, these
astonishing truthful statements …"

I like that.
but I have nothing to
say.

well, I do.
I tell her: "the red
sauce in the little bowl
is very hot so
don't use it unless you
like that sort of
thing."

—such statements don't
create a legend
but for ordinary mortals
they still have a
rather
sturdy
worth.

interview

what would you do if you had 5 minutes to
live? he asked.

nothing.

really?

yes, nothing.

all right, suppose you had 2
weeks?

nothing.

come on, don't say that, be
serious!

I think I
am.

all right, suppose you had 2
months?

either hold up a bank or take
up
water-skiing.

you're not being *serious*
about this whole
thing.

so I asked him:
what would you do
if you had 2 months to
live?

well, he answered, I'd
drink and fuck,

plenty.

o.k., put me down for
the same thing.

now you're talking!
he said.

for a man with 2 months to
live
he looked pretty
satisfied.

the lady who looks forever young

is in trouble:
the famous place she has gone to for all these
years for
face-lifts
refuses to give her
another:
the skin on her face is stretched so
tight
that she's like a balloon about to
burst
and they will not accept the
responsibility
of having her smile into another
camera
and exploding
like a tomato blasted by a
firecracker
all over the lens and all over
the people.

poor doll.
she's just another one of our
ageless
stars.
but have cheer: she'll never
die: film lasts longer than we
do.

an answer

within the past six years
there have been four
different rumors that I
have died.
I don't know who begins
these rumors
or why.
and certainly humans
do worse things than
this.
yet I always feel strange
when I must inform people
that I am
not yet dead.
somebody out there
or perhaps several
people
evidently get some
huge satisfaction
in announcing that I am
no longer
around.

some day,
some night
the announcement will be
true.
to put it mildly,
I am no longer
young.
but these death-
wishers
are an unsavory
group,
these hyenas,
these vultures,
these failed writers,
will also some day

be dead,
their petty bitterness,
their lying gutless
beings swallowed by
the dark.
but for the moment,
I am here
and these last lines
are for them:
your cowardice will
not be
missed
and you were
dead
long
before
me.

a model

I want to be like that
man who entered the
restaurant
tonight,
he parked right in
front
of the front
door.
blocking off a good many
parked cars,
then slammed his car
door shut,
walked in,
his shirt hanging out
over his big
gut.
when he saw the
maitre d', he
said, "hey, Frank,
get me a fucking
table by the
window!"
and Frank smiled and followed
him
along.

I want to be like
that man.
this way's not
working.

for over 70 years
now.

my companion

pissing in the toilet bowl
the centuries whirl past
me
and that lovely lady,
Suicide,
the only lovely
lady,
appears once again,
she knows me.
the walls are cream
yellow.

I flush,
return my penis to its
hiding place,
wash my foolish
hands,
walk from the
bathroom to this
room.

she has followed
me.

outside the night is
past midnight.
inside, there is no
time.

I uncap the beer
bottle,
swallow down
Rome,
Carthage,
yesterday and
the churning of
now.

she watches me
and waits.

I scratch my neck
as the entire
earth
comes in through
the window.
it has a form.
the form is a
body of dark
air.

the lady waits
for my love
as I notice the
hairs on my
arms,
the veins on
my hands.

I light a cigar,
inhale, then
exhale a cloud
of smoke.

I lift the beer
bottle
as somewhere
in the night
a dog barks
rapidly,
five times,
then
stops.

the barometer

when I was very young
I heard it from
my parents after they
discovered a few
early stories
hidden in my room:
"THIS IS UGLY!
THIS IS SHAMEFUL!"
I was finally
evicted from their
home
(which was
my first piece of good
luck).

then
after decades of
having my work
rejected
I had small bits
published
here and there
only to find many
critics totally
outraged
by my
efforts.

well, my parents
were dead,
they took the place
of my
dead parents.
I accepted the
justice of
this.

then I

married and
now I hear
my mother-
in-law
as she exclaims to
my wife:
"WHY DOES HE HAVE
TO WRITE THAT
WAY?
WHY DOES HE
DO IT?"

well, you know,
those voices
past and present are
always going to be
there.
or hopefully
they always will
be.

when they stop
I will know
that I have lost
my spirit,
I will know
I have lost
touch with the
direct line
to the mad
and
laughing
gods.
I will see my
photo on the
cover of
TIME
and I will be
taught in high
school English

along with
Hawthorne and
Whittier.

as long as the
mother-in-law
and many others
protest
I will know that
I am on the
trail of
a living and
lively
thing.

not that I write
in order to
create great and
ennobling
works
but if they
become so
and finally
silence
the grating
bellows of
idiots,
then let that
be
that.
fools sometimes create
genius by their
persistence
and their
puking empty
unjustified
horror,
unmitigated.

the rivers

the rivers of hell are mine, they aren't yours,
they're mine, flowing hot and dirty and
endless,
they're mine, all mine,
special,
for me,
nobody else,
they're mine
rushing me along,
night and day,
week after week, month after month,
year after year,
they're mine,
you hear me?

I no longer try to climb out,
I go with the rivers,
I talk to the rivers,
I tell them things
like,
"I know you.
we've been together a long
time.
I expect nothing
else."

we rush toward death
and neither of us
gives a damn about
death,
we've got our own game
going.

the rivers of hell are mine,
mine,
the rivers of hell
flowing
moving

with me,
my hells can only be
my hells,
if they're mine now and
maybe
forever,
so be
it.

dark, and darker

if I can find one hour of peace a day
I can survive.
that's one old-fashioned hour, 60 minutes,
one hour, please, let me have it now, today,
this day, this night, which is almost over.
let me have that hour, something is closing
in, fast.

what a horror show it has been, to have been
put upon the earth for this, it's unreasonable,
it's beyond
reason.

a screeching doom.

it began so long ago.

the room

nothing changes,
I am backed into this small room
like all the other small
rooms.

5 decades ago
I sat as a young man
before a machine,
the door closed,
the shades pulled
down.

now it is not the same
machine or
the same
young man.

the radio plays
and as I hit the keys
I recognize the classical
music,
I heard it half a century
before.

"peace and quiet are in
your future."
was the message in a
fortune cookie I opened
this week.
and I thought, maybe death
will be
that.

backed into this small room,
I make my last
stand.

the walls rise splendidly

up,
my cigarette smoke and
the music
rise.

the words bite into the
page.

my wrist watch on the
desk says
1:55 a.m.

the door is
open.

the two toughest

there's this big guy comes to see me, he sits in
this big chair and starts smoking cigars
and I bring out the wine
and we pour it down.
the big guy gulps them down and I gulp
right along with him.
he doesn't say much, he's a stoic.

when other people visit they say, "Jesus, Hank,
what do you see in that guy?"
and I say, "hey, he's my hero, every man has to have a
hero."

the big guy just keeps lighting cigars and drinking.
he never even gets up to piss, he doesn't have
to.
he doesn't bother.

he smokes ten cigars a night and matches me
drink for drink.
he doesn't blink.
I don't either.

even when we talk about women we
agree.

it's best when we're alone because he never
talks to the other people.

and I never remember seeing him
leave.
in the morning his chair is there
and all the cigar stubs and
all the empty bottles but he's
gone.

what I like best is he never disturbs the
image I have of him,

he's a tough son-of-a-bitch and I'm a
tough son-of-a-bitch
and we meet about once
every 3 months and put on our
performance.

anything more than that would
wipe us
both
out.

the darkening light

there are more and more
old people, middle-aged
people, young people,
children, babies,
deaths, marriages,
divorces, wars,
diseases,
sparrows,
songs,
cars,
you,
us,
me
sitting at a table ordering
this cup of coffee as the
mudlark
strangles.

those good people

the worst celebrities often support the most noble
causes,
some because so directed by their
publicity agents,
others, of the less famous
variety,
out of their need to be
accepted as good
souls.

beware these who rally too often to
popular causes,
not because the cause is
necessarily wrong
but because their motive is
self-serving—the cause being
their cause.
those people who swarm to
the ringing of bells and
speeches to the gatherings of
the righteously
indignant—
and often those who
ring the bells and give the
speeches—
are far worse as humans
than that or those they might
praise or support
or preach or rail
against.

think, would you want
one of these
smiling on your couch
on a rainy March night
or
any night
at all?

horse fly

the pimpled young man with his cap on backwards
came up to me at the racetrack
and asked, "who do you
like?" and I answered,
"don't you know that when you talk about that
the horse never
runs?"
he acted as if he hadn't
heard: "who do you like in the
exacta?"
"I don't bet exactas," I told
him.
"why?" he
asked.
"because they take 20 percent off
the top," I responded.
he acted as if that had nothing
to do with anything.
in a further effort to delete him from
the scene
I stated, "I don't bet daily doubles,
parlays, quinellas or
trifectas."
it was useless: "who do you like
in this race?" he asked
again.

"Your Mother's Ass,"
I informed
him.

as he checked his program
I walked
off.

night cap

there is no avenging angel or red burning devil
there is only me sitting here
at the age of 70
playing with the word.
I have been playing with the word for so
many decades now.
sometimes people see me on the street
and get excited.
"calm down," I tell them, "it's nothing."

the gods have been kind to me, being
neither in an institution or a
madhouse or a hospital.
considering all
my health is remarkably
good.
believe me, I had no idea I would
live this long, I had planned an
early exit and lived with a reckless
abandon.
don't be angry, I don't want to
hog the stage forever.
if somebody fairly good comes
along I will gladly step
aside.
I will write the stuff only for myself
and to myself,
which is what I have been
doing right along.

yes, yes, I've been lucky and
still am, and please be patient,
I will leave some day,
I will no longer defile these pages
with my raw and simple
lines.
I will become strangely quiet
and then you can

relax.
but for now, tonight, I am
working,
classical music is again on
the radio,
I square off with the
computer
and the words form and
glow on the screen.
son-of-a-bitch, you have
no idea, it has been a
wild and lovely
ride.

now I fill my glass
and drink to it all:
to my loyal readers
who have kept me off
skid row,
to my wife and my
cats and my editor
and to my car
which waits in the
driveway
to transport me to the
racetrack tomorrow
and to the last line
I will ever write.
it has been a miracle
beyond all
miracles.

"here's mud in your
eye!" as we used to say
in the thirties.

thank you.

action

I am upstairs in pajamas and bathrobe,
it is one a.m.
then I hear it: a woman screaming,
it sounds as if somebody is being
murdered,
there are thudding and crashing
sounds,
it's simply brutal,
I walk down the stairway and out
the front door.
my wife remains
inside.
I walk down the driveway to the
street.
it's across the street and 3 houses
down,
a red car appears to be parked
cockeyed, half in the drive, half
in the street,
the screaming continues
and the brutal sounds,
then the red car
veers around, points down the
hill and screeches
off.

the big kid from the corner
house
walks over to where I am
standing.
"what the hell's
happening?" I ask
him.

"some guy breaking all
the windows out of a
woman's car."

"holy shit."

the big kid had his car
shot full of holes
one night
about 6 months back
while he
slept.

the old neighborhood
is gone.

then a car roars out
of that same drive
backwards
and it goes
roaring up to the
top of the hill,
driving
backwards.

then it sits at the
top of the
hill
with the motor
running and the
lights
off.

the police arrive
then,
park their car outside
of that house,
red lights whirling.
they are talking to
some of the people
from the
house.

then the guy

at the top of the
hill
revs his engine
loudly,
slams it into gear
and roars
full speed
past the house and
down the
hill.

the cops jump into
their car,
more screeching,
it
flashes down
the hill
after him.

"nice to meet you,"
I tell the big kid,
"my name is
Hank."

"I'm Eddie."

we shake hands.

"gotta go, Eddie,
calm down my
wife…"

"me too, Hank,
watch your
ass."

"you too, baby."

I walk up the drive
and into the

house.

"what was it?"
she asks.

"love gone
wrong."

"anybody hurt?"

"I don't think so,
not yet."

I sit down on the
couch next to
her.
David Letterman is
on.

he doesn't know
what-the-hell about anything,
makes a face into the
camera.
I get up and go for
a bottle of
wine.

playtime

went to a Japanese restaurant with my
wife, she ordered tea.
I ordered beer in
the bottle, told the waiter, "no glass,"
and he stood there and asked,
"no glass?" and I responded,
"that's right."
some heads turned.
when the beer arrived I
lifted it and had a good hit.
the waiter came back again
and smiled, "no glass?"
"thank you," I said, "no glass."
then we ordered our meals.
when the waiter left my wife
said, "please get a glass, Hank."
"I prefer it this way," I said.
"I'm not going to be able to
eat," she said.
I lifted the bottle extra high,
held it like I was playing a
high note on a coronet,
had a good hit.
"you bastard," my wife
said.
I smiled.
god, I was bad.
and it was still only 9 p.m.
on a Sunday
night.
plenty of time to *really*
fuck up.
I
yawned.

poem for my 71st birthday

yes, I'm still here, doing about what I've always
done, although there are some moments of
hesitation
like I'll be at the plate and the big guy out
there will be about ready to fire one in
and I'll call time, step outside the batter's
box, knock some dirt off my cleats, look
around, there are sometimes blinding flashes of
light in my eyes
but I'll gather myself, shake it off, get back
in the box, feel the power returning, I
can't wait for the big guy's next pitch and it
comes in, a slider, bastard can't fool me,
I get the wood on it, it goes out of there,
way out of there and I trot the bases
as the young guys curse me under their
breath; too bad fellows, you see you
have to have a feel for it and as long as
it's there, you keep going, and when
you can't do it anymore, you'll still be
asking for one more turn at bat, just to
be there, even to swing and miss, it's the
doing that gets it done,
don't you understand this?

like this one here, it's probably only
a single or a short hopper to the
shortstop,
but I've had my swing
and I'll be back a few times
more,
the big guy doesn't have me
out of here
yet.

slow night

caught out of focus,
time is thin,
my slippers are
on,
the cats are asleep,
organ music on
the radio,
I light a cigar,
struggle for a
gentle
sanity.
I have eaten,
I have bathed.
the bottle is
unopened.

oh, if the boys
could see me
now.
or if I could see
them,
the "them" that
are left.

I will soon sleep,
my toes pointed
north.

tomorrow, if it
comes, could be
somewhat
better.

meanwhile, I
turn off the desk
lamp,
rise,
walk toward the

bedroom
followed by
1, 2, 3, 4, 5, 6, 7, 8, 9,
10, 11, 12, 13, 14, 15,
16, 17, 18, 19, 20,
21, 22, 23, 24, 25, 26,
twentyseven
28, 29, 30, 31, 32, 33,
34, 35, 36, 37, 38, 39,
40, 41, 42, 43, 44, 45,
46, 47, 48, 49, 50, 51,
52, 53, 54, 55, 56, 57,
58, 59, 60
sixtyone
62, 63, 64, 65, 66, 67,
sixtyeight
69, 70,
71
years.

to join the good wife
who endures
me.

the racetrack salutes you!

MILITARY DAY,
Sunday Sept. 8
FREE Grandstand Admission for
ALL Active Duty, Reserves, Retired,
Widows, Widowers & Dependents

Present I.D. at specially marked gates.

we hope you win
this time.

alone

if there were only some help from the
other writers, some lift, some gamble,
some fire,
but they are lax,
hang between nowhere and nowhere,
it hurts the head and the gut to
read them
and when I am feeling particularly
bad
as I am tonight
there's no place to go for a
boost or a laugh
or even a small
loan,
nothing to do but
pour another drink
look about the room
at anything—
a chair, a shoe, a box of
toothpicks,
I realize that there is
only one writer I can go
to,
he's got to do it for
me
once again,
get that line down
brisk and clean
to make the snarling women
laugh,
to make the lion turn in his
dream,
to make the dead armies
flower,
to become young again,
fresh as a lightning
flash,
to consume the monster

of sorrow,
to break horror with
just your
fingers, to
strangle the
darkness.

now
do it
do it

the gods are laughing
already.

the joke

it often happens when the party is
going well,
somebody will say, "wait a minute, that
reminds me, I heard this
joke, it will only take a minute and I
promise not to tell
more than one."

he leans forward and begins to tell
it, and this is the worst part because
you know it will not be funny, and even worse
than that, not even plausible, but he goes
on as your stomach feels as if you had
eaten a rotten egg, you reach the punch
line long before he gets to it, then he
finishes,
looks about.

there is silence, no laughter, not even
a smile.

"wait," he says, "don't you get it?"

"I understand," I tell him.

then he leans back, thinks that I
have no sense of humor, have had a
bad day, or that he has overestimated my
intelligence.

he could be right on all counts, I know
that I often watch famous comedians
who make millions tell awful jokes
while the audience roars with
appreciation and across the nation
numberless others join in from their
living rooms
as I sit there and think, this

stuff is bad, very bad, there's
little doubt about
it.

yet some drunk sits in a room
with me
and is offended because I
don't roll on the rug
when he lays a
dead egg that makes even
the gods
cringe.

but they are never offended
enough not to return
and toss in a new joke as bad
as the first, or worse,
returning *to* the first,
having forgotten the previous
agony.

in all my decades of joke-
listening
I've only heard one that is
worthwhile,
it goes like this—
no wait, I've forgotten
it.

you're
lucky.

Glasgow

do you mean in Scotland? he
asked.
I'm going to send some poems
there, I said.
you mean they have magazines
there? he asked.
yes, I answered,
writers and magazines
are everywhere, even your mother
is a writer and her ass is big and beautiful.
now wait a minute, he said.
I waited a minute.
I can take you, he said.
where? I asked.
all the way out, he said.
there's nothing between us but space,
I said, and if you want to close that
space, that's up to you.
you've got a big mouth, he said.
and your mother's got a great ass, I said.
why do you keep talking about my mother's ass?
he asked.
because that's all I see when I see her, I
answered.
they don't want your stuff in Scotland, he
said, they won't like it and I don't like it
either.

we were sitting at a table at the beach
on a windy Tuesday afternoon
and drinking green beer.
we were both writers but he wasn't as
good a writer as I was and it pissed him
off.

then his mother walked back to our
table and then she sat down with us.

she had been to the lady's room.

Mary, I told her, I'm going to send some
poems to Scotland.

order me another beer, she said.

I got the waiter's eye, he came over
and I ordered 3 more beers.

Mary spit on the floor and then
lit a cigarette.

Mary, I said, did anybody tell you
that you have beautiful eyes?
they glow like beacons in the
fog.

yeah? she said.

Mom, said the other writer, don't
believe anything he says.

but I do, she said.

Mary, I said, you've also got a
very beautiful ass.

and you've got a face like a
hyena, she said.

thank you, Mary.

it was a windy useless afternoon,
the seagulls were starving and
angry, they circled,
squawking, landing on the
sand, picking up uneatable
bits and then tossing them away, rising
again, flying, terribly beautiful

in an unreal sort of way and I
had half a chicken sandwich left,
I hurled it out the window and
the birds went for it, and the sea
kept pounding and the fish kept
swimming and we sat there with
our shoes on and our clothes on
and I was a
better writer than he but
that didn't take much and it didn't
really matter.
then Mary spilled her beer in her
lap,
got up and brushed herself off
with a napkin
and then I saw all that ass
again
as the waves roared and
I sat there with my biggest
hard-on since
1968.

owl

I saw an owl tonight.
I saw my first owl tonight.
he was sitting high on the phone pole.
my wife shined a light upon him.
he didn't move.
he just sat there
illuminated,
his eyes shining back.

my first owl.
my San Pedro owl.

then the phone rang.

we went inside.
it was somebody who wanted to
talk.
then they were finished.

we went outside and the owl
was gone.

damn the lonely people

I may never see an owl
again.

Dostoevsky

against the wall, the firing squad ready.
then he got a reprieve.
suppose they had shot Dostoevsky?
before he wrote all that?
I suppose it wouldn't have
mattered
not directly.
there are billions of people who have
never read him and never
will.
but as a young man I know that he
got me through the factories,
past the whores,
lifted me high through the night
and put me down
in a better
place.
even while in the bar
drinking with the other
derelicts,
I was glad they gave Dostoevsky a
reprieve,
it gave me one,
allowed me to look directly at those
rancid faces
in my world,
death pointing its finger,
I held fast,
an immaculate drunk
sharing the stinking dark with
my
brothers.

my computer

"what?" they say, "you got a
computer?"

it's like I have sold out to
the enemy.

I had no idea so many
people were prejudiced
against
computers.

even two editors have
written me letters about
the computer.

one disparaged the
computer in a mild and
superior way.
the other seemed
genuinely
pissed.

I am aware that a
computer can't create
a poem.
but neither can a
typewriter.

yet, still, once or
twice a week
I hear:
"what?
you have a
computer?
you?"

yes, I do
and I sit up here

almost every
night,
sometimes with
beer or
wine,
sometimes
without
and I work the
computer.
the damn thing
even corrects
my spelling.

and the poems
come flying
out,
better than
ever.

I have no
idea what causes
all this
computer
prejudice.

me?
I want to go
the next step
beyond the
computer.
I'm sure it's
there.

and when I get
it,
they'll say,
"hey, you hear,
Chinaski got a
space-biter!"

"what?"

"yes, it's true!"

"I can't believe
it!"

and I'll also have
some beer or
some wine
or maybe nothing
at all
and I'll be
85 years old
driving it home
to
you and me
and to the little girl
who lost her
sheep.
or her
computer.

thanks to the computer

you write a bad poem and you just
press the "delete" key and watch the
lines vanish as if they had never been,
no ripping pages out of the typer,
balling them up and tossing them into the
wastebasket.

the older I get the more I delete.
I mean, if I see nothing in a work, what
will the reader see?

and the computer screen is a tough judge,
the words sit and look back at you,
with the typewriter you don't see them
until you pull out the
page.

also, the keyboard on a computer is
more efficient than that on the
typer, with the computer the thoughts
leap more quickly from your mind to your
fingers, to the screen.

is this boring?
probably.
but I won't delete it because it isn't boring
me.

I am in love with THIS
MACHINE

see what it can do

now let's get back to

work.

safe

the house next door makes me
sad.
both man and wife rise early and
go to work.
they arrive home in early evening.
they have a young boy and a girl.
by 9 p.m. all the lights in the house
are out.
the next morning both man and
wife rise early again and go to
work.
they return in early evening.
by 9 p.m. all the lights are
out.

the house next door makes me
sad.
the people are nice people, I
like them.

but I feel them drowning.
and I can't save them.

they are surviving.
they are not
homeless.

but the price is
terrible.

sometimes during the day
I will look at the house
and the house will look at
me
and the house will
weep, yes, it does, I
feel it.

the house is sad for the people living
there
and I am too
and we look at each other
and cars go up and down the
street,
boats cross the harbor
and the tall palms poke
at the sky
and tonight at 9 p.m.
the lights will go out,
and not only in that
house
and not only in this
city.
safe lives hiding,
almost
stopped,
the breathing of
bodies and little
else.

3 blacks

it's midway through the card at the
track.
I am standing at a table,
getting my figures ready for the
next race.
I see them approaching,
coming down the
aisle.
the biggest one is
nearest me.
as he walks by
he gives me a bit of
elbow.
they keep walking on.
then the big one turns,
looks back
to see how I will react.
his face is blank as he
looks.
mine is blank.
he turns and walks on.

something about me bothered
him:
white skin.

brother, that's just the way it
is.

you drive a car?

what color is it?

don't blame the
car.

life like a big tender glove

old guy, small, maybe 67 but his hair is
pure white, it's the best part of him.
he carries coffee in a styrofoam cup.
he is moving toward his seat.
he is known to his seated compatriots.
"what I like about you fellows is you have a
sense of humor."
"screw you, Eddie," one of them answers.
he sits down with them.
"anybody here need a wife?"
"not yours, Eddie."
they are silent then.
it's 15 minutes to post time.
they study their Racing Forms.
all I can see from where I sit is the backs of
their necks, their old coats.
I don't know why but they remind me of
birds on a wire.
they are there 5 days a week.
God Bless America.
I get up and head toward the men's room,
thinking,
guess my father would have never guessed I'd
end up like this:
more stolid than the butcher,
more placid than a waiting deck of
cards,
not a button unbuttoned,
safe from the salt of the grumbling
sun.
yea, yea, yea.

the old guy in the piano bar

doesn't know how bad he is in that
white tablecloth place,
he's probably a relative of the
owner
and he sits at the piano and bangs
out
in the most obvious tired
manner
Jerome Kern or Scott Joplin
or Gershwin
and nobody ever applauds or
requests a tune,
they are into chewing or
conversation.

I don't feel sorry for him
and he doesn't feel sorry
for me
and part of his job is to
greet you when you
enter
looking up from his
keys
and to say
good night as you
exit
while still banging at
his keys.

but I do have a
fantasy
sometimes while
sitting at my table:
I see it all:
a stranger in a dark
overcoat,
fedora pulled
low over his

eyes
reaches into the
overcoat
and out comes a
.45
and he fires four
shots,
two into the piano
and two into the
player.
then it is silent.
the man rises slowly,
walks out and is
gone.

and the people
keep on talking and
laughing and drinking
and chewing
and the waiter walks
up and asks me,
"is everything all
right, sir?"

and I answer,
"everything is
beautiful."

"thank you, sir,"
he says and
walks off
as approaching
us
through the night is
the sound of a
siren.

nights and years

the days of hell arrive on schedule,
ahead of schedule.
and the nights of hell.
and the years of hell.

hell gnawing away like a rat
in your belly.

hell inside.
hell outside.

these poor words,
tossed into hell,
punched silly, sent
running.

I walk outside into the
night,
look up.
even the palm trees shriek
in agony.

the world is being pounded
by a senseless
force.

I go inside, shut the
door.

at this machine,
I write these words for
nobody.

the sun is dead.
the day is dead,
the living are dead.

only hell lives
on.

quiet in a quiet night

I can feel myself getting fat, old and
stupid.
I wheeze putting on my shoes.
I am no longer sure if I have years
left, months left, weeks left,
days left
or if the last minute is arrowing
in.
no matter.
this bottle of 1983
Saint-Emilion Grand Cru Classé
still rings the damned gong,
at least I've avoided sitting around
with the other old farts
sorting out unprecious
memories
the young are no help either,
they are shining mirrors without
reflection.

death sits in the chair across from
me and watches.
death sees but has no eyes.
death knows but has no mind.

we often sit together in the night.
death has one move left.
I have none.

this is an excellent wine.
it connects me with infinity.
a man without wine is like a fish without
water,
a bird without wings.

wine runs in the blood of the tiger
and me.

death is inferior
to this.
it can only win an obvious
victory.

death gets out of the chair and
stands behind
me.

it is a beautiful night.

I reach down and pull a long hair
from my forearm.
I touch it to my cigarette and watch
it sizzle away.

I am ripe.
the trees outside are silent.
there is no more,
no less.

a little cafe on 6th street

went in about 1:30 p.m.
ordered the turkey sandwich
on wheat plus some
decaf,
opened the paper and
waited.

two men to my left
talking:
"well, I wasn't going to
say anything but I looked at
your haircut and I saw
something was
wrong..."

"yeah, I was watching her
in the mirror and I thought,
'hey, what's she doing?'"

"I noticed it right
away...

you should have said
something..."

they went on talking about
the haircut and I went on
reading.

the sandwich and decaf
arrived with a side order
of
slaw and I began
eating.

"she should have taken more
off the *left* side..."

"yeah, yeah, she's always given
me a *good* cut before..."

"yeah, I mean, it doesn't look
bad but somehow it doesn't look
right, you
know?"

"I know...I might not go
back..."

then
one of the men
asked for some
cherry pie:

"I really like their
cherry pie..."

"me too...!"

I finished my meal
left the tip
got up and walked to the
cash register near the
door.

the men were into their
cherry pies:

"I wasn't going to say
anything, it's really not a
big *thing*, you know...but
I thought I'd better tell
you..."

"oh, I *knew*..."

"it'll grow out, you'll
be all right..."

"when it does, I don't think
I'm going back…"

"it's not that bad, it's
just…"

I paid and walked outside
and my car was there and
I got in and drove away
but I had to stop for a red
light
at Pacific
and
the turkey-on-wheat and
the slaw and the
decaf
huddled and bucked in
my stomach

and as I got the green light
I thought
I might not
go back there
either.

death in the modern age

I am writing a novel now and one way or
the other I have lost 4 chapters in this
computer.
now like everything else
this isn't such an important thing
unless it happens to
you.

like driving the freeway
you might see three or four cars
crashed and smoking
but the effect is only momentary.
in a few moments you are thinking
about something
else.

like you'll read this poem and
think, too bad, well, he lost 4
chapters
but couldn't he have written a
poem about
reaming some whore in a
motel room
instead?

pain seeks each individual
separately
and that's where hell
begins
stays
festers
celebrates
its
greatness.

now.

too hot

I am here courtesy of life,
sitting tonight, stiff-necked, weary;
95 degrees now
the cats will not come in,
there is no gunfire in the streets,
this whole town is roasting its ass,
the devils in Hell are sweaty;
there is screwing only in air-
conditioned rooms.
one a.m.,
no sleep, no dreams, and
the music from the radio limps
through the air.
even the dismally lonely forget to
phone.
that's the only good part of
this.
oh, there are other decent
parts:
at least the surgeon's knife is
not at work.
the flies zoom through the
fettered space
and there's no need to
continue writing this dripping
wet poem.
right?
right.

the last song

driving the freeway while
listening to the Country and Western boys
sing about a broken heart
and the honkytonk blues,
it seems that things just don't work
most of the time
and when they do it will be for a
short time
only.
well, that's not news.
nothing's news.
it's the same old thing in
disguise.
only one thing comes without a
disguise and you only see it
once, or
maybe never.
like getting hit by a freight
train.
makes us realize that all our
moaning about long lost girls
in gingham dresses
is not so important
after
all.

reunion

the cat sprayed in my
computer
and knocked it
out.

now I'm back to the
old
typer.

it's
tougher.
it can handle
cat spray, spilled beer
and wine,
cigarette and
cigar ashes,
damned near
anything.

reminds me of
myself.

welcome back,
old boy,
from the
old boy.

disgusting

I've got this large plastic floater with headrest
and I get onto it
and float about the pool
looking up at the tall majesty of the trees
through the unclear California air
I paddle about searching for
different views.
some of my cats
sitting at the edge of the pool,
stare,
thinking that I have gone
crazy.
maybe I have.
they are used to seeing me
sleeping or
at the computer
they don't mind
that.
but this?
have I turned into a
fish?
or what?

I flip off my floating bed,
sink down into the blue
pool,
rise up,
swim to the
edge.

I climb out,
walk toward my
towel.

dinner soon
and the boxing matches on
tv,
later a bottle of

cabernet.

it's so nice, this
road to
hell.

Bach, come back

sitting in this old chair, listening to Bach,
the music splashes across me, refreshing, delightful.
I need it, tonight I feel like a man who has come back
from the same old war, death in life,
as my guts say not again, not again, to have fought
so hard for what?
too often, the only escape is sleep.
Bach saves me, momentarily.

so often I hear my father laughing, the dead laughter
of the father who seldom laughed in life
is laughing now.
then I hear him speak: "You haven't escaped me.
I appear in new forms and work at you through
them.
I'm going to make sure that hell never stops for
you."

then Bach is back.
Bach couldn't you have been my father?
nonetheless, you make my hell
bearable.

I have come back from suicide, the park bench, it was a
good fight
but my father is still in the world,
he gets very close at times
and suicide creeps back into my brain,
sits there, sits there.

as old as I have gotten,
there is still now no peace,
no place,
and it has been months since I,
myself, have laughed.

now Bach has stopped
and I sit in this old chair.

old man, old chair.

I still have the walls, I still have my
death to do.
I am alone but not lonely.

we all expect more than there
is.

I sit in undershirt, striped pants, slippers.

hell has a head, hell has feet and a mouth,
hell has hair and nostrils,
hell curves down and encircles me
and I think of bridges, windows,
buildings, sidewalks,
last New Year's Eve,
an eyeball in the sand,
the dogs, the dogs, running in this
room now,
eight of them,
nine of them,
many of them,
coming closer and closer,
I watch them,
I wait,
old in my slippers,
something cutting through me,
the dark night humming and
no laughter,
no laughter
ever
again.

the modern life

just lost another poem in this
computer.
I don't believe it was
immortal.
neither was this day
or night.
not when all you
can remember
is the 4 horse breaking
through the gate
and spilling the jock
in the yellow silks
as the man
in front of you
bit into a hotdog
like a mongrel
dog
as the market went
down
and Van Gogh
up.

mailbag

a schizophrenic
in Dallas
writes me about his
problems:
he
hears voices,
he's
hooked on
Beckett,
also his shrink
makes him
sit too long
in the waiting
room.

he's supported
by his
mother
and he follows
women's
softball.

also he recently
won
2nd prize
in a chili
cook-off.

you ought to come
to Austin,
he writes,
you'd love
Austin.

I file his letter
in with the
other letters
from schizophrenics.

I've been to
Austin.

self-invited

well, strap my ass on backwards, phone China,
run the birds off the wire,
buy a painting of a red dove and remember
Herbert Hoover.
what I am trying to say is that 6 nights out of the
last 8 there have been visitors, all self-invited, and
like my wife says, "we don't want to hurt their feelings."
so we have sat and listened to them, some
famous and some not so, some fairly bright
and entertaining, some not so
but it all ends up as chatter, chatter, chatter, voices,
voices, voices, a polite heady whirl of sound and
there's a loneliness there: they all want to be accepted
in one way or another,
they want to be listened to, and that's understandable but
I am one of those human beings who would rather sit quietly
with my wife and 6 cats (or I like to sit upstairs alone
doing nothing).
the idea is that I am selfish and that people
diminish me; the longer I sit and listen to them
the more empty I feel but I don't get
the idea that *they* feel empty, I feel
that they enjoy the sound from their
mouths.

and when they leave almost all make a little gesture
toward a future visit.
my wife is nice, makes them feel warm as they exit, she's
a good soul, so good a soul that when, say, we eat out and
choose a table she takes a seat where she can "see the
people" and I take a seat where I can't.

all right, so I was forged by the devil: all
humankind disinterests me and no, it's not fear although
certain things about them are fearful, and it's not
competition because I don't want
anything that they want, it's just that
in all those hours of

voices voices voices
I hear nothing either essentially kind or daring or noble,
and not the least bit worth all the time shot through
the head.

you can remember when you used to run them out into the
night instead of letting them wind themselves
down,
those with their lonely wish for company, and you are
ashamed of yourself for putting up with their mostly pure
crap
but otherwise your wife would say
"do you think that you are the only person living on
earth?"

you see, that's where the devil's got
me.

so I listen and they are
fulfilled.

old

I see the old men at the racetrack, they are bent, carry
canes, their hands tremble, I ride up the escalators with
them.
we don't speak.
I am older than most of them and I wonder why
the lights are out for them?
do they still hope to win the Pulitzer Prize or to cup the
breasts of young maidens in their
hands?
why don't they just finish and die?
I'm ready to go any damned time, I'll even take them
with me, 2 or 3 of them, or a half-dozen, a dozen:
their wrinkled white skins and their ill-fitting
dentures,
let them stiffen up and clear the space for clean
fresh lightning!
what good to linger?
for the bedpan last chapter?
for the nurse with the television mind, half the weight
of her body in flanks and buttocks?

why honor the old?
it's just the stubbornness of genes, a trick to keep
a void existing.
almost all have lived lives of obedience and
cowardliness.
why not honor the young?
their lives are just beginning to rot.
why honor anybody?
but, please, not the old.

in the next war the old should fight the old
while the young drink and dream and
laugh.

these old fucks
betting two dollars to show
at the racetrack.

it's like being dead and rolling over
in the grave to find a more
comfortable
position.

the young poets

the young comfortable poets send their work to
me,
usually 3 or 4 very short
poems.
some are fairly able,
but they lack the
texture of madness and
gamble,
the inventiveness of the
wild and the
trapped.

there is a comfort there
which
disconcerts.

then there is the work
of the Street Poets.
being on the skids, they
should have some
life advantages, they
should not be debilitated
by
pretense.
but they are full of
it.
most of their output is
about how they are
not
recognized, that the
game is
fixed,
that they are truly
the great
ones
and they go on
about
that, while writing

little of anything
else.

each week
one or two little
packets arrive
from either the
Street Poets or
the comfortable
poets.

kindness does not
work with either
group.

any response to
their work
begets more
work
plus their
long letters
expounding
against the
fates
as if nobody
but themselves
ever had to
deal with
them.

and if you fail to
respond to
that, in most cases,
there will be
subsequent
letters
which rail against
your
inhumanity:
you *too* are

against them,
and, fuck you,
buddy,
you've lost
it,
you never had
it,
fuck you!

I am not an
editor.
I never mailed my
work to anybody
but an
editor.
I never read my
work to wives or
girlfriends.

these poets apparently
believe it's all
politics, an in-
game,
that some word
from you
will enable them
to become
renowned and
famous.
and that's what
they
want.
that.
and only
that.

the packets of
poems keep
arriving.

if I were an editor
I'd have to
reject most of
them.

but I'm not.

I write poems
too.

and when some of
them come back
and I reread them
I usually feel that
they *should* have
come back.

what you have to do is
dig
in,
beat that keyboard
so that it yells and
sings and laughs so
hard
that the fix gets
unfixed, that the god-
damned miracle
arrives
splashed across the
paper as you get up
and walk across the
room, your head
buzzing, your heart
wanting to fly
through the
ceiling.
it's the best
fight, the last
fight, the only
fight.

Belfast

writing a letter to Belfast
to somebody who reads my
books.

somehow it seems odd to
write a letter to
Belfast
but everything is odd
these days
very
like writing books
or sitting here
in striped pants and
slippers at
12:30 a.m.
without even
thinking
as my young wife is
out somewhere
enjoying herself
as young wives
should
do.

the dream

I continually have dreams of being lost, of asking
directions
but the people I ask have an indefinite way about them, or
they act as if they would rather not be bothered
but finally one of them will give me confusing
and misleading directions.
I follow the directions but they lead
nowhere: strange hills and curling freeways, and I
have no idea where I am.
at times I will be walking, at other times I will
be driving my car
or finally I will lose my car and then I
will ask other indefinite and misleading
people
where is my car?
and they will give me vague answers,
they won't say, we don't know where your car is, they will
pretend that it is not missing or they will refuse to tell me
where it is.

then I will give up on the car, I want only to return
to where I live but the people I ask will give me more
unreal directions
until I finally give up on them.

I walk and walk along, it is always broad daylight, just before
noon but as I walk I do not recognize any of my
surroundings.
the air seems very bright and clear but it also seems
somehow false
as I walk and walk along.

when I awaken I feel much
better, of course.
I know where I am, here is the bed, the walls,
here is my wife in bed next to me.
and I think, well, there it was, the same
dream.

over and over again.

I get up and go to the bathroom, look in the mirror,
scratch myself, come back out.

and then, strangely enough, in a short while the dream is almost
forgotten.

returning to an old love

well, here the computer is down again for
the count and I am back with the good old IBM electric.
it really doesn't matter as long as I have something
to get the word down with.
I get physically and mentally ill when I am
locked away from the
word,
and at least the IBM—
this machine—doesn't suddenly gulp pages
and pages of words
that you have celebrated the hours with,
words that vanish
forever.

this machine is slow but safe
and I welcome it back like the good friend it still
is.

I hope that it forgives me
and arranges more good luck for me.

now it's balking a bit,
looking me over.

come on baby, I say,
do it.
do it again.

I'm sorry about that whore,
you warned me about her
but I wouldn't listen.

now we're back together.
come on, baby,
do it
again.

be a lady
tonight.

cool fur

one of our fattest
cats
CRANEY
sleeps on his back
just about
anywhere
his legs sticking up
into the air.

he knows that we will
never step on
him
but doesn't know
how nervously
and incompletely we
humans
sleep.

and live.

old?

I'll be 73 in August,
almost time to pack my bags for a
lark in the dark
but there are two things
holding me back:
I haven't written enough
poems yet
and there's this
old guy who lives in
the house next door.
he's still there and he's
96.
he knocks on his window
with his cane and
blows kisses to my
wife.
he's totally alert,
straight arrow back,
quick on his feet,
he watches too much
tv but don't we
all?

I visit him sometimes.
he talks away,
not bad stuff, he sometimes
tends to repeat himself
but it's almost worth hearing
a second time.

I was sitting with him one
day and he said,
"you know, I'm going to
kick off soon..."

"well," I said, "I don't know
about that."

"I do," he said.
"now look, would you like
to trade for my house?"

"well, yeah, it's a nice place."

"I don't know if you can give me
what I want for it ..."

"well, I don't either, try me."

"well," he said, "I'll trade for a new
set of testicles."

when this guy dies there is
going to be a great big space
that is going to be hard
to fill.

you know what I
mean?

a problem

we met for dinner
at a place near the
harbor.
Paul, his wife,
Tina.
me, my wife,
Sarah.

we finished
dinner.
I suggested
drinks at our
place.

they followed
our BMW in
their
Mercedes.

with our drinks
we got into
politics and
religion.
I looked at
Paul and
noticed that
his face had
turned into a
cardboard
face, his
eyes into
marbles.

then I saw
my face
in the mirror
above the
mantle.

I had the
head of an
alligator.

I poured
more
drinks.

the conversation
turned to the
after-life,
abortion and
the Russians.

then somebody
told an
ethnic
joke
and the night
was over.

we walked them
to the
door.
they got into
their Mercedes
and backed out
down the
drive.

we waved
they blinked
their
lights.

we went
back
inside.

"I wonder what

they are saying now
about
us?" I
ventured.

"what are we
going to say
about
them?" Sarah
asked.

"nothing," I
answered.

"did you ever
notice?"
she asked.

"what?"

"sometimes you
have
a head
like an
alligator."

"I've noticed."

"we don't have
any friends
at all,"
Sarah
said.

taken

Ezra, Celine, Hamsun, Sartre, others
got mixed up with that whore
Politics
and it makes you wonder,
was it bad diet?
bad liquor?
ennui?

couldn't they have just motored
down the coast and stopped off
for a simple lunch?
why assume other roles?
fools run governments, not every-
one can guide the
world.

centuries don't change men,
they only make them seem more
foolish.

those writers, couldn't they have
gone boating?
couldn't they have skipped the
idiot's trap,
the total loss of
sense?

how could they have done so
well
and then so
badly?

why exchange a gift from
the gods for a handful of
dung?

such beautiful men
self-castrated

as if they couldn't bear
their grand luck,
retiring to the dumb
dark
before it reached
them.

welcome darkness

the door closes and you
grin at
death.
all pretense is gone
now.
what remains is
the similarity of night
and morning;
the victimization of
time and
space;
the befuddled
proclamations;
the borrowed
assertions;
the righteous
enactments;
the camouflage;
a common
denominator.

the oldest horror
show.

the murder of the
sun.

the last of
life.

Bach

I'm
listening to a work of his
recorded in
1923.
I was 3 years old
then
but Bach was
ageless.

I am soon going
to die
but I feel no
remorse about
this.

Bach and I are
in this
room
together.

his music now
lifts me beyond
pain
and my
pathetic
self-
interest.

Bach, thanks to you,
I have no
living
friends.

great jazz

you keep getting an idea
that something is going
to happen,
you can feel it in the
edge of your
fingernails
it's climbing the
walls
as the jazz group keeps
working,
going from one chorus to
the next,
just sliding, rising,
it's a sweet hustle,
you drink without getting
drunk,
smoke endless
cigarettes at your
corner table.
the energy keeps
building.
smoke, drink and
listen.
the city is here,
the world is
here.
if there's an answer,
it's here.
god damn.
shame to leave
even to piss.
you hold it.
something's going
to happen.
it's like the 20s in
Kansas City.
baby, baby, I'm
going to stay here

forever,
they're going to
have to slide my
bones off this
chair,
it's happening,
it's happening,
at
last, at last, at
last …

a moment

for Wagner the gods of Valhalla also burn in the
flames,
as here tonight
I am sober,
my horse won the last race
as I was driving in on the freeway;
it is the somber time just before
midnight,
Wagner roaring out of the
radio,
I have come to pause
before the agony and the magic
of another man,
long dead,
he's here with me
now,
it's frightening and
wonderful,
then one of my cats walks
in,
looks at me from the
floor
with his glorious
eyes,
he then leaps up on the
desk
and stands before me,
Wagner bouncing
off of him
and I reach out
and touch the
cat.

impossible.

wondrous

all right, lay on the rain.
lay the rain on.
lay it on.
on the roof.
I hear it on the roof.
I know that it soothes
old wounds and
new.
then too,
one always remembers
the times when there
was no roof
and it
rained.
one does not forget
that.

it will rain all this
night
and we will sleep
transfixed by the dark
water
as our blood runs through
our fragile
life.

lay the rain on.

the divine
broth.

fact

careful poetry
and careful
people
last
only long
enough
to
die
safely.

there

the centerfielder
turns
rushes back
reaches up his glove
and
snares the
ball,
we are all him for
that moment,
sucking the air
into our
gut.
as the crowd roars like
crazy
we rifle the ball back
through the
miraculous
air.

PHOTO: Claude Powell

CHARLES BUKOWSKI is one of America's best-known contemporary writers of poetry and prose, and, many would claim, its most influential and imitated poet. He was born in Andernach, Germany, to an American soldier father and a German mother in 1920, and brought to the United States at the age of three. He was raised in Los Angeles and lived there for fifty years. He published his first story in 1944 when he was twenty-four and began writing poetry at the age of thirty-five. He died in San Pedro, California, on March 9, 1994, at the age of seventy-three, shortly after completing his last novel, *Pulp* (1994).

During his lifetime he published more than forty-five books of poetry and prose, including the novels *Post Office* (1971), *Factotum* (1975), *Women* (1978), *Ham on Rye* (1982), and *Hollywood* (1989). Among his most recent books are the posthumous editions of *What Matters Most Is How Well You Walk Through the Fire* (1999), *Open All Night: New Poems* (2000), *Beerspit Night and Cursing: The Correspondence of Charles Bukowski and Sheri Martinelli, 1960–1967* (2001), and *Night Torn Mad with Footsteps: New Poems* (2001).

All of his books have now been published in translation in over a dozen languages and his worldwide popularity remains undiminished. In the years to come Ecco will publish additional volumes of previously uncollected poetry and letters.